3. 75

61.7495 (9-13-68)

THE POLITICAL TESTAMENT
OF CARDINAL RICHELIEU

THE POLITICAL
TESTAMENT OF
CARDINAL
RICHELIEU

THE SIGNIFICANT CHAPTERS
AND SUPPORTING SELECTIONS
TRANSLATED BY
HENRY BERTRAM HILL

THE UNIVERSITY OF WISCONSIN PRESS · MADISON, 1961

Published by The University of Wisconsin Press,
430 Sterling Court, Madison 6, Wisconsin

Copyright © 1961, by the Regents of the
University of Wisconsin

Printed in the United States of America
by Vail-Ballou Press, Inc., Binghamton, New York

Library of Congress Catalog Card No. 61–7495

INTRODUCTION

Armand Jean du Plessis, Duke of Richelieu and Cardinal of the Roman Catholic Church, the most important single figure in the building of French absolutism, was born and died in the parish of St. Eustache in Paris (1585–1642). He was a younger son of an impecunious nobleman from Poitou who had risen to the rank of Grand Provost in the service of Henry III, the last Valois king of France. Intended for a military career, he dutifully agreed to abandon it to support his widowed mother by fulfilling the family claim to the bishopric of Luçon, replacing an older brother who had belatedly chosen the cloister. After lengthy and serious theological studies the young candidate journeyed to Rome where the pope, impressed with his intelligence and demeanor, granted the necessary dispensation and invested him with his episcopal office in 1606, several years before he reached the canonical age. Soon after, he entered upon the active administration of his diocese, one of the meanest in the country. With what was to become his customary thoroughness and attention to detail he undertook its physical and spiritual refabrication, and before long he had established a reputation as a promising young clerical administrator. In 1614, as a representative of the clergy to the Estates General he won the attention of the Queen-Mother, Marie de Médicis, and shortly thereafter he became a Secretary of State. Fortune turned briefly against him in 1617, however, when the Queen's favorite, Concini, was assassinated at the command of the adolescent Louis XIII, but Richelieu was recalled from disgrace and exile by the distraught king who wanted the Bishop to mediate in his ever-recurring conflict with his mother. For this and other services Richelieu won first the cardinalate (1622) and then, having finally completely subdued the last of the king's suspicions, the helm of state as prime minister (1624).

Once in office, it was Richelieu's program to make Louis the unquestioned master of his realm, and France preëminent in Europe. Although he could be both devious and harsh, he preferred the method of subtlety, and he skillfully practiced the art of the possible. He created no new instruments of government and he propounded no systematic theory of state; rather, he treated each problem in the context of his long-range purposes. If one approach seemed inappropriate at the moment, he held it in reserve while trying another. If nothing worked he waited for conditions to change. The only fixed aspects of his policy were his utter determination and patience. His first completed objective was the destruction of the political privileges (but not the religious immunities) of the Huguenots, symbolized by his successful siege of the fortified Protestant port city of La Rochelle and sealed by the tolerant Edict of Alais (1629). He followed this victory by continuing a relentless attack upon all nobles high and low who defied the will of the King, which also meant, needless to say, Richelieu's own will as well. In 1627 he insisted upon the execution of the Seigneur de Bouteville, a noble braggart who flamboyantly fought a preannounced and forbidden duel on the Place Royale. The same fate was meted out in 1632 to the Duke of Montmorency, a highly placed and popular nobleman of ancient family who headed a revolt in Languedoc. He kept Gaston of Orléans, the King's scapegrace brother, under constant threat for his intrigues, and he even drove the troublesome Queen-Mother, his one-time protector, out of the country. With the king supreme at home, Richelieu in 1635 carried France into the Thirty Years' War (1618–48). Although a cardinal of the Church, he supported the Protestant side, for his purpose was to destroy the power of the Hapsburg states, Austria and Spain, which had so long encircled and threatened France. More than any other individual he was responsible for turning that war from a predominantly religious struggle into a predominantly political one. He died in 1642 before the war was over and won, but not before the outcome he wanted had been shaped, and not before he had provided in Cardinal Mazarin a successor capable of carrying his will to its conclusion. By 1659, when Spain as well as Austria acknowledged defeat, France, strongly absolutist at home, had emerged as the dominant state in Europe.

For a man who was both so busy and so frequently ill, Richelieu left a considerable body of writings. This work ranged from plays (the Cardinal was extremely vain about them, and one, *Mirame*, was at least passable in quality) to the *Mémoires du cardinal de Richelieu* compiled posthumously from his papers by Harley de Sancy, Bishop of St. Malo.[1] Other parts may be found in his *Lettres, instructions diplomatiques et papiers d'état du cardinal de Richelieu*, edited by Georges Avenel.[2] Lastly, there is his *Testament politique*, which has a special interest and usefulness of its own. More needs to be said about it specifically, if for no other reason than because unlike the rest of Richelieu's writings it has been much abused, misunderstood, and even neglected. Indeed, the two things long most widely known and said of it were both in complete error: that the book was a forgery, and (by some of those who accepted its authenticity) that it outlined Richelieu's plan for an aggressive foreign policy at Germany's expense.

[1] 10 volumes, Paris, 1907–31.
[2] 8 volumes, Paris, 1853–77.

Before discussing what the book is *not*, however, it
might be well to deal with what it *is*. As Richelieu himself tells us at the beginning of the *Political Testament*, it
had been his intention from the first moment of his ap-
pointment to compile a detailed history of the time of
Louis XIII, designed in part to glorify his reign, in part
to instruct his successors. Coming to realize, however,
that his limited time and strength would prevent the ful-
fillment of this hope, Richelieu decided upon the more
modest objective of a book of observations and maxims
for the king's guidance should fate still the cardinal's
hand. Running to some 360 pages in the best French edition, it is divided into two parts. The first, largely retro-
spective in nature in spite of several of the chapter head-
ings, is concerned with the history of the earlier portion
of the reign of Louis XIII and with the institutions of
French government and society; the second, more hor-
tatory and prospective, deals with public policy. At times
fragmentary, at others repetitious, the work is almost
always pithy and frequently pungent. Richelieu was not
a great speculative genius—not a new Machiavelli—but
he was an observant, shrewd, even cunning, and certainly
highly successful administrator. His text breathes the
atmosphere of this experience and although the reader
may not accept the underlying philosophy, he is forced
to agree that the cardinal-minister generally knew in
great detail and depth what he was writing about.
Whether or not the king ever read the *Political Testa-*

ment we do not know; probably not, for he followed his minister in death in a few months. Had Louis XIII read it, however, he would have found a most revealing and devastating character study of himself, a portrait stern but not unkindly in tone, because Richelieu had a real, albeit guarded affection for his master, and his words were meant to reform, not to anger. There is, in this regard as well as in other matters, what might even be called a sort of winsomeness in the writing of this apparently icy man; and there is also a slightly pathetic tone, doubtless in part genuine, in his description of the burdens and rewardlessness of high office. Indeed, the most enduring single impression to be gained from the *Testament* is the unintended self-portrait of its author—friendless, lonely, selfless, severe, distrustful, inflexible, indefatigable, devoted only to the welfare of the state as he saw it.

It is easy for us to see now why the *Political Testament* was long considered by many to be spurious.[3] Of the seventeen existing manuscript copies, no two agree and none can be directly attributed to Richelieu on its own textual merits. No version can be considered a finished literary product, yet none contains more than one or two passing references to events after 1638, four years before Richelieu's death. The work was first published

[3] For a discussion and bibliography of the investigation of the question see E. Préclin and V. Tapié, *Le XVIIe siècle* (2nd ed.; Paris, 1949), pp. 180–81, and Rémy Pithon, "A propos du testament politique de Richelieu," *Schweizerische Zeitschrift für Geschichte,* VI (1956), 177–214.

only some four decades later, in 1688, by a foreign press
in Amsterdam.

All of these matters can now be quite convincingly explained.[4] Like the rest of Richelieu's formal writings,
the *Testament* was in fact based on notes and succinct
précis written or dictated at odd moments, either for
some matter of passing importance or for future refer-
ence, and ultimately assembled by another hand, in accordance with his suggestion. There was once some reason to believe that in this particular case the work of
editing was accomplished by Richelieu's alter ego, Father
Joseph, whose own death in 1638 is also close to the ter-
minal date for the historical contents of the *Testament*.
Now it is thought, however, that like Richelieu's *Mémoires*, the *Political Testament* was compiled after his
death, perhaps about 1646, by one or more of his secre-
taries and drawn from manuscripts mostly but not exclu-
sively from his pen or dictation.[5] The cardinal himself,
we may be sure, never completed the final literary composition of the text—it is much too rough. Although in
certain passages perhaps he felt directness of statement
was more important than polish, since he intended the
Testament only for the eyes of the king and not the world
at large, there is greater likelihood that his attention
turned to more pressing duties and he simply failed to

[4] A more extended account may be found in the eighty pages
of introduction to the book cited in footnote 12.
[5] Pithon, *op. cit.*, pp. 197–98.

polish his thought and expression. As for its publication, there was little point to putting it into print following the death of both master and servant. Cardinal Mazarin, Richelieu's successor, had enough troubles of his own without reminding the French of his predecessor, while Louis XIV, later, would hardly have deemed it expedient to publicize the maxims of a man whose policies were in certain respects so different from his own. Indeed, when the *Testament* finally did see the light of day, it appeared in The Netherlands, under Protestant auspices, and was intended to serve as an attack upon the religious intolerance of Louis XIV.[6]

While early doubters of the genuineness of the book included Richelieu's first serious biographer,[7] it was Voltaire who gave real notoriety to the issue.[8] With even more than his customary vigor and tenacity he went at the subject time and again. He based much of his criticism on the contents of the *Testament*, rejecting both its intrinsic worth and its purported authorship. While in doing this he was doubtless swayed by the belief that the book was not diabolical enough to be the work of a

[6] Cardinal de Richelieu, *Testament politique* . . . (Amsterdam, 1688). The publisher was Henry Desbordes, a Protestant émigré from Saumur. There were a number of reprintings, including several pirated ones.

[7] A. Aubéry, *Histoire du Cardinal Mazarin* (2 vols.; Paris, 1688). There could, of course, be no mention of it in his *Histoire du Cardinal de Richelieu* (Paris, 1660).

[8] Voltaire, *Oeuvres complètes* (52 vols.; Paris, 1877–85), XIV, 22–23, XXI, 328, XXXV, 207 and 290, XLV, 550, XLVIII, 215.

priestly despot, he did point out many of its errors and inconsistencies. For more than a century his views heavily colored the judgment of many scholars who, since they did not know as much as we do about its actual composition, tended to feel like their opponents that the text had to be accepted or rejected in its entirety. Unfortunately, support was given to Voltaire's contentions when, in the midst of his polemics and because of them, a second edition was brought out in 1764, this time in France.[9] The editor, hoping to improve upon the not grossly inaccurate first edition, actually incorporated considerable erroneous and even extraneous material and took unconscionable liberties with several of the indisputable passages. [Through the years, understandably, *Validity* there were grounds for a lingering suspicion about the genuineness of the *Testament*.[Then, in 1880, Gabriel Hanotaux,[10] the author of Richelieu's most exhaustive biography,[11] found in the Bibliothèque Nationale a collection of key Richelieu documents which established

[9] Cardinal de Richelieu, *Maximes d'état ou testament politique* . . . , F. Marin, ed. (Paris, 1764).

[10] G. Hanotaux, "Maximes d'état et fragments politiques de Cardinal de Richelieu," *Mélanges historiques*, III (Paris, 1880), 705–822.

[11] G. Hanotaux, *Histoire du Cardinal de Richelieu* (6 vols.; Paris, 1893–1947). The latter part was completed by the duke de la Force. Most readers will prefer C. V. Wedgwood, *Richelieu and the French Monarchy* (London, 1949), which is brief and informing, or the somewhat fuller and equally popular K. Federn, *Richelieu* (London, 1928).

beyond all reasonable doubt both the authenticity of at least considerable portions of the best existing manuscripts and the closeness of the cardinal to their actual composition. More recently, on the basis of Hanotaux's discovery, Louis André prepared a critical edition of the *Political Testament*.[12] Except for one incomplete version,[13] there have been, therefore, only these three French editions in as many centuries. Abroad, there were early and complete translations into Spanish [14] and English,[15] the latter, and presumably the former, from the Amsterdam version. More recently a German translation was made of parts of it.[16]

[12] Cardinal de Richelieu, *Testament politique*, L. André, ed. (Paris, 1947). Regrettably, this edition too is not above some small suspicion. Originally it was greeted with fulsome praise.—R. Mousnier, "Le testament politique de Richelieu," *Revue historique*, CCI (1949), 55–71. Later, Mousnier discovered several scholarly lapses. —*ibid.*, CCII (1949), 137. Only those specializing professionally in textual criticism, however, need to feel concern. Except for minor refinements we probably have as good a text as we will ever have, and all competent authorities agree on its general authenticity.

[13] R. Gaucheron, ed., *Oeuvres du Cardinal de Richelieu* (Paris, 1947).

[14] *Testamento politico*, Juan de Espinola Baeza, trans. (Madrid, 1696).

[15] Cardinal de Richelieu, *The Compleat statesman; or, the political will and testament, of that great minister of state, Cardinal Duke de Richelieu* (London, 1695). This translation is both highly inaccurate and archaic. Contrary to the statement of Mousnier, *Revue historique*, CCI (1949), 55, copies may be found in the libraries of the University of Wisconsin and Yale University, if not elsewhere.

[16] Cardinal de Richelieu, *Politisches Testament und kleinere Schriften*, F. Schmidt, trans., and W. Mommsen, ed. (Berlin, 1926).

Validity [margin note]

The question of the general authenticity of the *Testament* having at long last been resolved, there remains that second piece of misinformation to deal with—the charge that in this book Richelieu elaborated an expansionist foreign policy predicated on the prevention of German unification. The truth of the matter is that neither in the *Political Testament* nor elsewhere did Richelieu develop such a plan. The nearest thing to possible support for the contention is to be found in the contemporary work of a Jesuit father, who reported that Richelieu had once said he wished to reëstablish the natural frontiers of ancient Gaul. There was, it must be admitted, a certain plausibility to the supposition from the German viewpoint in the light of the over-all diplomacy and outcome of the Thirty Years' War, but there is absolutely no supporting documentary evidence of merit, and much, including the *Testament*, which points to the contrary.[17]

The translation which follows has been made from the André edition.[18] Every effort has been made to be *style* [margin note]

[17] André (p. 66) implies that this myth finds its main strength in German prejudice. One must admit there is a certain stubbornness in the work of even as good a scholar as W. Mommsen, whose more recent introduction to the translation cited in footnote 16 is little different in tone from his own earlier *Richelieu, Elsass und Lothringen; Ein Beitrag zur elsasslothringischen Frage* (Berlin, 1922). André, however, takes much too seriously F. Grimm, *Das Testament Richelieu* (Berlin, 1941), which is nothing but a rabid and openly Nazi tract.

[18] For which acknowledgment is here given for the kind permission of the publisher, Editions Robert Laffont, 30, rue de l'Université, Paris (VIIe).

Validity's
footnotes

faithful to the original—always to the spirit and usually
to the letter. The few footnotes are aimed only at supply-
ing the necessary minimum of clarifying information;
anyone with deeper curiosity should turn to André's full
annotations. The complete text has several lean and repetitious sections which do not warrant translation and
these have been eliminated. What remains, however,
does ample justice to Richelieu's intent. As the table of
contents to this book indicates, of the eight chapters in
Part I, all but one (Chapter V, which is brief and concerned largely with obscure administrative matters) are
given at least in part, and the most significant portion,
Chapters VI and VII, is reproduced in full; while the
ten chapters of the highly important Part II are given
in their entirety save for Chapter IX, from which several
parts were omitted because they were filled with minute
and unimportant details. The longest omissions—the
"Succinct Narration" in Chapter I of Part I and the eco-
nomic sections in Chapter IX of Part II—are the least
interesting and among the most closely questioned, both
as to authenticity and, particularly for the passages on
economics, as to Richelieu's competence to speak in-
formatively. In sum, therefore, what is presented here
is probably as close as we can come to the real substance
and the best of the *Political Testament*. In reading it, one
can see an experienced and tireless administrator pa-
tiently employing examples in the forms of historical
analogies and political aphorisms, often repeated again

Style

and again with only slight variation, in the hope—if necessary from the grave—of convincing, cajoling, even frightening Louis XIII into being a great king—a greatness he achieved only to the not unpraiseworthy degree of granting unflinching support to a great minister when he found him.

CONTENTS

Part II

THE POLITICAL TESTAMENT
OF CARDINAL RICHELIEU

THE POLITICAL TESTAMENT

OR MAXIMS OF STATE OF

CARDINAL RICHELIEU

To the King

Sire:

When it was first Your Majesty's pleasure to give me a part to play in the management of your affairs [1] *I determined to devote my fullest efforts to the completion of your plans, so perfectly designed for both the welfare of the state and the embellishment of your reign.*

God having so blessed my intentions that the success and happiness of Your Majesty have become the wonder of this age, as they will certainly be the admiration of the next, I felt it incumbent upon me to write the history of your most successful reign. This would have saved from oblivion an account of the many events worthy of living forever in the memories of men, and could also

---

[1] Richelieu became the principal minister of Louis XIII in 1624 and continued in this office to his death in 1642.

have served as a guide to the future. *No sooner had this thought occurred to me than I began to act upon it, believing that I could not commence too soon that undertaking which would be finished only with my own death. I carefully assembled not only the material for such a history; what is more, I made a draft of part of it, covering several years, substantially in the form in which I intended to publish it.*

But I must confess that there is more sense of accomplishment in making history than in writing about it, although there is not a little pleasure in reporting that which was often brought about with great difficulty. No sooner had I begun to enjoy the pleasures of this undertaking, however, than the continuous illnesses and inconveniences which the weakness of my constitution and the burden of public affairs inflicted upon me [2] forced me to abandon it as too great an extra burden. Thus reduced to the extremity of not being able to carry out in this regard that which I fondly hoped to accomplish for the glorification of yourself and the welfare of your state, I thought the least I could do, without incurring God's punishment, was to leave to Your Majesty certain thoughts on what I consider most important for the proper governing of this kingdom.

Two considerations urge me to undertake this work. The first is the fear and hope I have of finishing my days before yours run their course. The second is the faithful

---

[2] The Cardinal never enjoyed good health.

desire I have for the protecting of the interests of Your Majesty which not only makes me want to see them crowned with success during my lifetime, but which also induces me to hope for their continued fruition after the inevitable tribute exacted by fate from each of us prevents me from witnessing them any longer.

This effort will see the light of day under the title of Political Testament *because it is designed for use after my death for policy-making and the management of your realm, if Your Majesty deems it worthy of such use. It will contain my latest thoughts on these subjects, which will surely be the best legacy within my capacity to leave Your Majesty when it pleases God to call me from this life.*

I will present it in the briefest and most precise fashion possible, and by so doing follow both my own inclination and my natural style of writing—thereby accommodating myself as ever to Your Majesty's love for getting to the point with the fewest possible words, your interest being in the substance of things rather than in the long discourses with which most men clothe what they have to say.

I would esteem myself extremely fortunate if, after my death, my spirit as reflected in these memoirs could contribute even in a small way to the governing of this great country in whose direction you were pleased to give me a part to play far beyond my merit.

With this in mind, and knowing with what success it

has pleased God in the past to favor the decisions Your Majesty has reached in collaboration with your most faithful servants, I rest confident you will be influenced by what advice I can provide for your future.

.   .   .   .

This account will be made in such faithful conformity with the best contemporary historical evidence that all will believe that the advice I give to Your Majesty has no purposes beyond the welfare of the state and in particular of yourself, of whom,

Sire,

I am the ever humble, faithful, obedient, devoted and thankful subject and servant.

Armand, Cardinal Duc de Richelieu

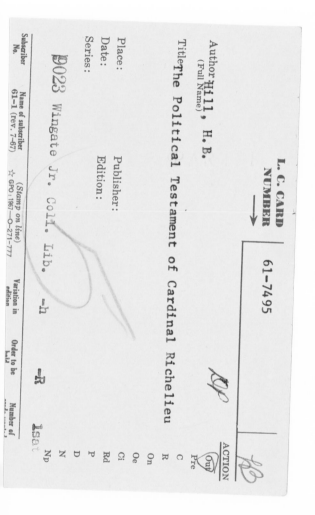

L. C. CARD
NUMBER
→

61-7495

Author Hill, H. B.
(Full Name)

Title The Political Testament of Cardinal Richelieu

Place: Publisher:
Date: Edition:
Series:

B023   Wingate Jr. Coll. Lib.   —h   —R   1sat

ACTION

Pre
C
R
On
Oe
Ci
Rd
P
D
N
Np

CHAPTER I

GENERAL STATEMENT

OF THE ROYAL

PROGRAM

When Your Majesty resolved to admit me both to your council and to an important place in your confidence for the direction of your affairs, I may say that the Huguenots shared the state with you; that the nobles conducted themselves as if they were not your subjects, and the most powerful governors of the provinces as if they were sovereign in their offices.

I may say that the bad example of all of these was so prejudicial to the welfare of this realm that even the best courts were affected by it, and endeavored, in certain cases, to diminish your legitimate authority as far as it was possible in order to carry their own powers beyond the limits of reason.

I may say that everyone measured his own merit by his audacity; that in place of esteeming the benefits which they received from Your Majesty at their proper worth, they all valued them only as they satisfied the demands of their imaginations; that the most scheming were held to be the wisest, and often found themselves the most prosperous.

I may further say that foreign alliances were scorned, private interests being preferred to those of the public, and in a word, the dignity of the royal majesty was so disparaged, and so different from what it should be, because of the misdeeds of those who conducted your affairs, that it was almost impossible to recognize it. It was impossible, without losing all, to tolerate longer the conduct of those to whom Your Majesty had intrusted the helm of state; and yet everything could not be changed at once without violating the laws of prudence, which do not permit the passing from one extreme to another without preparation.

The bad state of your affairs seemed to force you to precipitate decisions, without a choice of time or of means. And yet it was imperative to make a choice of both in order to profit by the change which necessity demanded of your prudence.

The best minds did not think that it would be possible to pass without shipwreck all the rocks in such uncertain times. The court was full of people who censured the temerity of those who wished to undertake a reform, and all well knew that princes find it easy to impute to those who are near them the bad outcome of the undertakings upon which they have been well advised. So few people, consequently, expected good results from the change which it was announced I wished to make, that many held my fall assured even before Your Majesty had elevated me.

Notwithstanding these difficulties which I explained to Your Majesty, knowing how much kings may do when they make good use of their power, I dared to promise you, with assurance, that you would soon find remedies for the disorders in your state, and that your prudence, your courage, and the benediction of God would give a new aspect to this realm. I promised Your Majesty to employ all my industry and all the authority which it should please you to give to me to ruin the Huguenot party, to abase the pride of the nobles, to bring all your subjects back to their duty, and to restore your reputation among foreign nations to the station it ought to occupy.

.   .   .   .

In broadest outline, Sire, these have been the matters with which Your Majesty's reign has thus far been concerned. I would consider them most happily concluded if they were followed by an era of repose during which you could introduce into your realm a wealth of benefits of all types. In order to present the problem to you, it is necessary to look into the nature of the various classes in your realm and the state which it comprises, together with your own role, both as a private and a public person. In sum, what will be indicated is the need for a competent and faithful council, whose advice should be listened to and followed in governing the state. It is to the detailed explanation and urging of this that the remainder of my testament will be devoted, divided for order and clarity into several chapters and sections.

CHAPTER II

THE REFORMATION OF THE

ECCLESIASTICAL ORDER

One could write whole books on the subject of the various classes of this realm.[3] My objective, however, is not that of most others who content themselves with describing all of the factions of a country without considering whether or not the public derives any benefit from the description. Rather, I will try to present to Your Majesty in a few words what is most important for the establishment of the well-being of all your subjects, whatever be their station.

When I remember that in my youth I saw noblemen and other lay individuals hold "in confidence" [4] not only the greater part of the priories and abbeys, but also parishes and bishoprics, and when I also consider that in

[3] The traditional pattern of three classes—ecclesiastics, nobles, and commoners—is followed, this chapter being concerned with the first of these.

[4] A scheme by which a layman could acquire part of the income of a position in the church.

13

my early years of service license was so widespread in the monastic communities of both men and women that scandals and bad practices prevailed where one would expect to find only the quest for spiritual edification, I avow that I derive not a little consolation from the realization that those abuses have been abolished during your reign, and that now appointments "in confidence" and other malpractices in monastic matters are as rare as legitimate possession and good conduct were then. In order to sustain and extend this blessing, Your Majesty should, in my opinion, take great pains to fill all bishoprics with persons of both real merit and commendable habits, and to give abbeys and other simple benefices at your disposal only to candidates of recognized probity, frowning publicly on all those holding ecclesiastical positions who act licentiously and punishing in exemplary fashion those churchmen whose actions are scandalous.

. . . .

. . . . learning, one of the greatest adornments of nations, should be spoken of in this chapter because its achievements are to be attributed to the church, since so many of its truths bear a natural relationship to the sacred mysteries which divine wisdom has entrusted to the care of the ecclesiastical order.

Because a knowledge of letters is entirely indispensable to a country, it is certain that they should not be indiscriminately taught to everyone. A body which had eyes all over it would be monstrous, and in like fashion so would be a state if all its subjects were learned; one would find little obedience and an excess of pride and presumption. The commerce of letters would drive out that of goods, from which the wealth of the state is derived. It would ruin agriculture, the true nourishment of the people, and in time would dry up the source of the soldiery, whose ranks flow more from the crudities of ignorance than from the refinements of knowledge. It would, indeed, fill France with quibblers more suited to the ruination of good families and the upsetting of public order than to doing any good for the country. If learning were profaned by extending it to all kinds of people one would see far more men capable of raising doubts than of resolving them, and many would be better able to oppose the truth than to defend it. It is for this reason that statesmen in a well-run country would wish to have as teachers more masters of mechanic arts than of liberal arts.

.   .   .   .

It seems to me, in fact, when I consider the great number of men who profess to teach and the multitude of pupils they instruct, that I see an infinite number of sick people who wish only to drink pure clear water for their cure but are pressed by a thirst so consuming that they down uncritically all that is presented to them. Most of them as a result drink impure concoctions from what are frequently unclean containers, thereby increasing their thirst and illness rather than assuaging either. Indeed the great number of schools ineffectively operating in so many places has given rise to two evils. One, of which I have just been speaking, consists of the mediocre capacity of those who teach, there being an insufficiency of candidates properly qualified to fill the available posts. The other arises from the lack of natural talent for letters among many of those whose parents urge them to study, without any examination of their aptitude, because of the convenience of the facilities. These are the reasons why almost all of those who go to school acquire only a smattering of letters, some because they are capable of no more, others because they have been badly taught.

While this bad situation has serious consequences, the remedy is simple. The only thing necessary to do is to reduce all the schools, except in the greater cities, to three or four classes—just enough to raise the young from the grossest ignorance, which is a hindrance even for those going into the army or into commerce. By this means, before anything is finally determined, two or three years of schooling will make known the degree of the pupils' intelligence. It will then be possible to select the promising ones who, sent on to the great cities, will have a better chance at success since they will have an aptitude more suited to letters and will henceforth be instructed by better teachers.

Having thus provided a defense against that evil,

which is greater than it first appears, it is still necessary to guard against another to which France would indubitably succumb if all the existing schools were under a single hand. The universities believe that they have been done a great injustice in not being left, to the exclusion of all other agencies, the sole privilege of instructing the young. The Jesuits, on the other hand, would not be unhappy to be the only ones employed in that function. Reason, however, which should prevail in all sorts of differences, cannot permit the denial to an established possessor of that possession to which he has title, nor can the public interest allow an association as renowned as that of the Jesuits for both its piety and its principles to be deprived of a function in which it is able to perform such a useful service for the public. If the universities should control all teaching, there would be reason to fear that they might in time return to their old pridefulness, which could be as damaging in the future as it was in the past. If, on the other hand, the Jesuits did not have to share the instruction of the young, then one could expect not only the same misfortune—one could indeed expect several others in addition.

An association which is governed more than any other has ever been by the laws of prudence and which gives itself to God without depriving itself of the knowledge of the things of this world lives in so perfect an inner working harmony that it acts with unusual singleness of purpose. When such an association also submits itself by

a vow of blind obedience to a perpetual head it should
not, following the laws of sound policy, be allowed to
have much authority in the state. Indeed, any association
so powerful could be a great threat, particularly if it is
true, as indeed it certainly is, that one is naturally pleased
to advance those from whom one has received his first
instruction. There is the further fact that parents always
have a particular affection for those who have performed
these services for their children. It is also true that one
cannot entrust the entire education of young men to
Jesuits without running the risk of giving them a power
most dangerous to a country because all its influential
positions and offices would ultimately be filled by their
members or those over whose minds they had gained an
early ascendency, often of lifelong duration. If one adds
that the administration of the sacrament of penance gives
to that association a second ascendency over all sorts of
persons, which certainly is not of less significance than
the first, if one considers that by these two means they
can penetrate the most secret plans of individuals and
families, it would be impossible to conclude otherwise
than that they ought not to be the only ones given the
responsibility here discussed. These reasons have been
so persuasive in all countries that none to date have
turned over the empire of letters and the entire instruction of their youth to this association alone.

·   ·   ·   ·   ·   ·   ·   ·   ·   ·

Also, since the frailty of the human condition requires a counterweight in all things, which is, indeed, the
foundation of all justice, it is most reasonable that the
universities and the Jesuits should teach in emulation of
each other, so that the competition might stimulate their
virtue. The prosperity of the sciences would then be all
the more assured to the country because if they are in
the care of two guardians, one could carry on if the other
should lose sight of its sacred charge.

. . . .

CHAPTER III

THE REFORMATION OF

THE NOBILITY

After having presented what I feel to be absolutely necessary for the restoration of the first order of the realm, I pass to the second, noting first of all that it is necessary to realize that the nobility is one of the principal organs of the state, capable of contributing much to its preservation and stability. For some time now, however, it has suffered at the hands of public officials made ever more numerous at its expense by the misfortunes of these times, and there is great need of supporting it in its struggle with these people. The opulence and pride of the officials enable them to take gainful advantage of the nobles, rich only in a courage which leads them freely to proffer their lives to the state.

While it is necessary so to support the nobles against those who would oppress them, it is also necessary to see that they in turn do not exploit those beneath them. It is a common enough fault of those born to this order

to use violence in dealing with the common people whom
God seems to have endowed with arms designed more
for gaining a livelihood than for providing self-defense.
It is most essential to stop any disorders of such a nature
with inflexible severity so that even the weakest of your
subjects, although unarmed, find as much security in the
protection of your laws as those who are fully armed.

. . . .

While the nobility merits to be generously treated if
it does well, it is necessary at the same time to be severe
with it if it ever fails in what its status demands of it. I
do not hesitate to say that those nobles who, degenerat-
ing from the virtuous conduct of their forebears, fail to
serve the crown constantly and courageously with both
their swords and their lives, as the laws of the state require, deserve the loss of the privileges of their birth and
should be reduced to sharing the burdens of the common
people. Since honor should be more dear to them than life
itself, it would be much more of a punishment to them
to be deprived of the former than the latter.

. . . .

However, nothing must be overlooked in sustaining
the nobles in the great virtues of their fathers, and
neither should anything be omitted to help them enlarge
the landed estates which they have inherited. . . .

. . . .

The Means of Preventing Duels

There have in the past been so many edicts issued with the unfulfilled hope of preventing duels that it is difficult to know just what to do to put an end to the continuation of this plague. Frenchmen hold their lives in such contempt, as we know from experience, that the extreme penalty has not always been the best one with which to curb their frenzy. They have often fancied that it was even more glorious to violate such edicts, demonstrating by so extravagant a gesture that they valued honor above life itself. But on the other hand the possibility of losing their earthly possessions, without which they cannot be happy in this world, outweighs the threat of dying bereft of the grace of God so necessary to prevent unhappiness in the next, and makes the fear of being deprived of their offices, property, and liberty a more efficacious restraint upon their spirits than that of losing their lives.

I have overlooked nothing which could possibly help in the search for a proper remedy for this pernicious evil. I have even sought to find out if the king could confine the issue to the two principals in order to prevent a general battle of seconds and to decide in this way the difference which had caused the taking up of arms, thereby avoiding the multiplicity of duels which occur daily. I had believed there was every likelihood that one

could by this means free France of this disastrous mad-
ness, since permission for such combats could come only
from the decision of judges to whom the contenders had
submitted their claims for an assessment of the serious-
ness of the offense. It seemed safe to assume that this
would have prevented many duels, since there really are
few quarrels which cannot be ended by a reasonable
agreement. I add, in support of this idea, that formerly
such duels were permitted both in this realm and in several others. I believed that one could by this method
abolish the use of the barbarous practice of insisting that
every offended man must seek justice for himself and
find his satisfaction in the blood of his enemy. But, after
having read and reread several times all that the most rec-
ondite authorities had said and written on this highly
important subject, to say nothing of the advice of the
least squeamish and most resolute theologians, I discovered that kings, being established to protect their subjects and not to destroy them, could not endanger their
subjects' lives except for some public good or special
necessity. They cannot, indeed, permit private combat
without exposing the innocent to the same fate as the
guilty, and, seeing that God is not obliged to make right
ever victorious, the outcome of a trial at arms is uncertain. Further, although permission had sometimes been
granted for such duels in several countries, even with
the approval of the local churches, the results were so

harmful, and so clearly so, that finally the Church Universal forbade and condemned the practice under the greatest penalties.

I have come to realize that there is a great difference between on the one hand making two individuals fight to avoid a general battle and so finish a war, and on the other of making them fight to prevent a duel. The first is permissible because nature teaches us that the part should be exposed for the whole, and reason indicates that the individual should risk himself for the generality. In addition to the fact that this policy has been followed many times in the past, one can also find examples in holy writ of instances where the results were beneficial and clear, saving the lives of a great number of persons who then could live to serve the public on later occasions. But it is not the same with the second, which by its nature is illicit in that in place of the certain protection of the generality at the risk of a few individuals, thereby preventing a great evil at the cost of a small one, it definitely risks the loss of individuals in exchange for an imagined utility which is not founded on a firm basis. This policy is also the less acceptable since in place of stopping the practice of dueling it could augment the license, because the pride of the nobility is so great many would feel that to ask for limited combat by this method would really be seeking an excuse for not fighting at all, with the result that vanity would take a shorter route to the rectifying of its injuries and the giving of proofs of its

courage. The late king in 1609 tried to adopt this means
of limitation, along with all of the necessary measures to
make it effective: deprivation of property, offices, and
life for those who fought without first obtaining permission. But it was useless, and this is what obliged Your
Majesty, after having tried the same policy at the beginning of your reign, to have recourse by means of
your edict of the month of March, 1626, to the other
remedy which has had great effect since the penalties,
although moderate, yet weigh more heavily on those who
consider their lives as worth less than their property or
their liberty.

But, because the best laws in the world are useless if
they are not inviolably observed and because often those
who fall into this kind of crime use so many artifices to
hide the evidence, which then becomes almost always
impossible to substantiate, I do not hesitate to tell Your
Majesty that it is not enough to punish the authors of
known challenges and duels by the full weight of your
edicts. On the contrary, when there is substantial evidence even without tangible proof, you should appre-
hend all offenders and imprison them at their own expense for a period commensurate with the particular
circumstances of their offenses. Furthermore, the negli-
gence in beginning prosecution which ordinarily char-
acterizes your attorney generals, the laxness of your
courts, and the corruption of the times are such as to
indicate that everyone esteems it as great an honor to

aid those who are in conflict to conceal their crime as
true gentlemen would hold such action to be as dishon-
orable as the hiding of the loot of a thief, thereby ren-
dering your edicts and your guardianship useless. In such
cases, when the way of action is the only means of making your edicts and ordinances observed, your authority
entitles you to go beyond the ordinary forms of law and
discipline. Without such a recourse the state could not
expect to last, and it actually provides your officials with
a means of punishing in a legal fashion since in all likelihood they can find the source and proof of a crime when
the suspect is under arrest, while if he were free he could
make every effort to destroy the evidence.

If, finally, Your Majesty decrees that the seconds in
duels are as culpable as those they second and are liable
to the same penalties until the principals have surrendered
themselves and are duly punished, then you will probably have done all you can to stop the course of this frenzy,
and the care which you take to preserve the lives of your
nobles will render you master of their hearts, arousing
in them a fidelity so firm that they will eagerly fulfill all
the tasks you choose to assign to them.

CHAPTER IV

THE REFORMATION OF

THE THIRD ORDER

OF THE REALM

For the purpose of covering the Third Order of the Realm methodically and to present clearly what it is necessary to do to keep it in the condition in which it ought to be, I will divide the subject into three parts. The first will deal with the body of judicial officers; the second, with those in charge of finances; the third, with the common people, who bear the full expenses of the state.

The Judiciary

It is much easier to recognize the faults of the judicial system than to prescribe the remedies. There is no one unaware of the fact that those officers whose positions have been established to weigh all things evenly have themselves so heavily loaded one side of the scales to their private advantage that no balancing is now possible.

· · · · · · · · · · ·

The view of the vast majority of people is that the sovereign remedy consists in the suppression of the sale and heritability of offices, and the awarding of them without charge to persons of an ability and probity so well known that their merit can never be questioned by even the most envious. But, since this is not something which can now be inaugurated and would be difficult to introduce at any time, it would be useless to propose means aimed at its accomplishment.

·   ·   ·   ·   ·   ·   ·   ·   ·   ·

In any event, although it is almost always dangerous to be dogmatic in giving one's advice, I must say emphatically that in the present state of affairs, as well as in what seems likely to be the situation in the future, it is better, to my way of thinking, to continue the sale and heritability of offices than to alter radically the whole establishment.

·   ·   ·   ·   ·   ·   ·   ·   ·   ·

There is no question but that the suppression of the sale and heritability of offices would conform with both reason and all concepts of good government, but the inevitable abuses which would result from the distribution of appointments on the simple basis of the king's wishes and consequently on the favor or cunning of those most influential with him, makes the present system more tolerable than the appointive one which formerly prevailed

and whose inconveniences would be as evident now as
they were then.

.   .   .   .

If you show favor to those officers of justice whose
reputation is good, if you frown upon those who, destitute of merit, have only the money necessary to qualify
for the judiciary, if you deny your approbation entirely
to and properly punish those who, abusing their power,
sell justice to the prejudice of your subjects, you will
be doing absolutely all that can be done of a practical
nature for the reformation of this body. Just as in the
case of the ecclesiastical order, everything depends more
on those who administer it than upon the laws and regula-
tions, which will remain useless if those responsible for
their execution do not have the necessary good intentions.

Finance Officers

The financiers and tax farmers compose a group apart,
prejudicial to the best interests of the state, but nevertheless indispensable.[5] Their public employ is an unavoid-
able evil, and it is imperative that their activities be con-

[5] Much of the revenue of the kingdom was derived from in-
direct taxes collected by bankers known as tax farmers. These taxes
were let by contract, the bankers making a profit from the collect-
ing service. In addition, the government frequently borrowed
money by one device or another, again to the profit of the bankers.

fined to the barest minimum. Their excesses and the corruption which has arisen among them have grown to the point where they can no longer be suffered; they cannot aggrandize themselves further without ruining the state, or for that matter, without ruining themselves, for they have provided enough evidence to justify the confiscation of the excessive wealth they have amassed in a short time. This can be easily verified by comparing what they possessed at the beginning of their operations with what they will be found to have since acquired.

I well know that such a procedure can be subject to great misinterpretations and that it can serve as a pretext for unjust actions, and I have not touched upon this point in passing with the idea of advising the practice of something so drastic. But I maintain that no one could justly complain if one governed with such circumspection that in punishing all quickly enriched schemers no harm were thereby done to those who had acquired wealth and power by virtue of their honest efforts, surely a most innocent means of self-improvement. The same is true for those who receive gifts due to the favor of their master, or as a natural recompense of their public services. This, too, is not only irreproachable, it is most legitimate, since in addition to being pleasing to the beneficiaries it is also advantageous to the state, which is always better served when those who serve it are well treated.

.   .   .   .

After having given serious thought to all conceivable remedies for the thorny problems created by financiers, I conclude that the best thing to do is to reduce their number to the smallest possible, and to substitute for their use in important public matters the temporary employment of men of known good repute and capability. This is better than to establish such persons in titled positions they feel allow them to rob with impunity.

.   .   .   .

The People

All students of politics agree that when the common people are too well off it is impossible to keep them peaceable. The explanation for this is that they are less well informed than the members of the other orders in the state, who are much more cultivated and enlightened, and so if not preoccupied with the search for the necessities of existence, find it difficult to remain within the limits imposed by both common sense and the law.

It would not be sound to relieve them of all taxation and similar charges, since in such a case they would lose the mark of their subjection and consequently the awareness of their station. Thus being free from paying tribute, they would consider themselves exempted from obedience. One should compare them with mules, which being accustomed to work, suffer more when long idle than when kept busy. But just as this work should be reasonable, with the burdens placed upon these animals proportionate to their strength, so it is likewise with the burdens placed upon the people. If they are not moderate, even when put to good public use, they are certainly unjust. I realize that when a king undertakes a program of public works it is correct to say that what the people gain from it is returned by paying the *taille*.[6] In the same fashion it can be maintained that what a king takes from the people returns to them, and that they advance it to him only to draw upon it for the enjoyment of their leisure and their investments, which would be impossible if they did not contribute to the support of the state.[7]

I also know that many princes have lost their countries and ruined their subjects by failing to maintain sufficient military forces for their protection, fearing to tax them too heavily. Some people have even fallen into slavery under their enemies because they have wanted too much liberty under their natural sovereign. There is, however, a certain level which one cannot exceed without injustice, common sense indicating in each instance the proportion which should prevail between the burden and the ability of those who sustain it. This consideration

[6] The *taille* was the principal tax, varying from place to place in France both as to its base and its burden, and was levied largely on the lower class.

[7] As elsewhere in this chapter, Richelieu in some confusion tends to lump together all segments of this very heterogeneous class. It is also apparent that his sympathies for lesser folk were not profound.

ought always to be religiously observed, although a prince cannot be esteemed good just because he taxes his subjects no more than necessary, nor considered evil because occasionally he takes more.

Also, just as when a man is wounded, his heart, weakened by the loss of blood, draws upon the reserves of the lower parts of the body only after the upper parts are exhausted, so in moments of great public need the king should, in so far as he is able, make use of the abundance of the rich before bleeding the poor heavily. This is the best advice Your Majesty can follow, and it is easy to put into practice since in the future you will draw the principal income for your state from the general tax farms, which are much closer to the interests of the rich than of the poor, since the latter, spending less, contribute less to the total.

CHAPTER VI

THE ROLE OF

THE KING

God is the principle of all things, the sovereign master of kings, and the only one who can make their reigns happy. If the devotion of Your Majesty were not known to all, I would begin this chapter, which is concerned with your person, by stating to you that should you not follow the wishes of your Creator and submit to His laws you could not hope to have yours observed by subjects obedient to your orders.

But it would be a superfluous gesture to exhort Your Majesty in the matter of devotion. You are so bent toward it by inclination and so confirmed in it by virtuous habit that there is no reason to fear you might turn away from it. It is because of this that in place of showing you the advantage religious principles have over others I will content myself with observing that although devotion is necessary for kings, it ought to be devoid of all over-scrupulousness. I say this, Sire, because the sensitiveness

of Your Majesty's conscience has often made you fear
to offend God in reaching even those decisions which
you cannot abstain from making without sin.

I well know that faults of such a nature in a prince are
much less dangerous for a state than those which lean
in the direction of presumption and disrespect toward
that which a monarch should revere. But since they are
faults, it is necessary to correct them, as it is most certain
that they have resulted in many inconveniences prejudicial to the interests of the state. I beseech you, in this
matter, to try to fortify yourself against your scruples,
reminding yourself that you can never be guilty in the
eyes of God if, on occasions involving difficult discus-
sions of matters of conscience, you follow the advice of
your council, confirmed by that of several competent
theologians not suspected of having an interest in the
question.

This basic problem recognized, there remains nothing
else of a personal nature intrinsically necessary to the
successful conducting of your affairs save the preservation of your health, and I cannot go on without giving
it special emphasis.[8] Long, thorough, and persistent observation of your conduct in all sorts of circumstances
emboldens me to say that nothing is more important than
the proper direction of your will, which otherwise can
be a most powerful enemy, as it so often is with princes

[8] In point of fact, Richelieu here begins his penetrating and often
merciless probing of the king's character.

who cannot be prevailed upon to do not only what is useful but what is even absolutely necessary. Your Majesty's mind so completely dominates your body that the slightest emotional upset affects your whole being. Many occurrences of this have made me so certain of the truth of my diagnosis that I am convinced I have never seen you ill in any other way.[9]

God has seen fit to give Your Majesty the force of character necessary to act with firmness when confronted with business of the greatest importance. But as a balance to this noble quality He has often allowed you to be sensitive to matters so small that no one in advance would suspect they might trouble you and thus try to protect you from their bothersomeness. So far, time alone has provided the only remedy for these overwhelming experiences of which the inward consequence has always been a bodily indisposition. You are, in this regard, much like those whose great courage makes them disdain the blows of a sword but who cannot, because of a certain natural antipathy, stand the puncture of the scalpel. It is impossible for many men to anticipate the surprises which will come from their emotions. I do not think, however, that such is the case with Your Majesty, who has many excellent qualities most people do not have. I believe that, in all likelihood, the first ebullience of your ardent youth having passed, the stability of a greater maturity will help you protect yourself by forethought

[9] Louis XIII was a chronic victim of enteritis, from which he ultimately died at the age of 41.

in the future from an enemy which is all the more dangerous because it is internal and domestic, and which has already caused you misfortune serious enough on two or three occasions to have brought your life in jeopardy.

Just as this is a matter of great importance for your health, so is it also for your reputation and glory, for which it should always appear that reason prevailed over your emotions. I cannot help repeating again a plea I have made many times before to Your Majesty, begging you to apply yourself to the matters of greatest importance to your country, disdaining the little ones as beneath your thought and interest. It would be useful and inspiring for you to dwell often upon the vast prospects of the trend of events. If you preoccupy yourself with the small matters, you will not only fail to gain benefit therefrom, you will even bring misfortune upon yourself. Not only does such a preoccupation divert you from a better one. Just as little thorns are more capable of pricking than larger ones, which are more easily seen, so it would be impossible for you to protect yourself from many unpleasant happenings inconsequential for public business and bad for your own health.

The great emotional outbursts to which you have been subject on several occasions urge me to tell you here, as I have earlier done more than once, that while there are certain public charges necessary to the furtherance of state affairs which you must perform, there are others the performance of which can do no less than destroy the good disposition of whoever plunges into them. This in turn so adversely affects those charged with carrying out decisions that they too are less able to do what is expected of them. The experience of governing that Your Majesty has acquired from a reign which thus far has lasted twenty-five years [10] makes you well aware of the fact that the outcome of large undertakings rarely conforms directly with the orders initially given. It also teaches you that you might better have compassion for those charged with the execution of your commands when their efforts do not succeed, rather than to blame them for the poor results for which they may not be responsible. It is only God whose acts are infallible, and yet His goodness is such that, letting men act as their weakness directs, He even so overlooks the gulf between their deeds and His standards. This should teach kings to tolerate with patient reasonableness what the Creator endures assuredly because of His benevolence.

Your Majesty being by nature delicate, with a weak constitution, and a restless, impatient disposition, particularly when you are with the army where you always insist on taking the command, I believe it would be committing a crime if I did not beseech you to avoid war in the future in as far as it is possible.[11] This plea I base

---

[10] Which places the date of the writing of this part in 1635.

[11] If the date given above applies here, Richelieu was speaking on the eve of France's entrance into one of its most extended and fateful military ventures, the Thirty Years' War.

upon the fact that the frivolousness and unreliability of
the French can generally be overcome only by their
master's presence and that Your Majesty cannot, without endangering your health, commit yourself to a program of long duration with the hope of success. You have
made the valor and strength of your arms well enough
known to entitle you in the future to think only of how
to enjoy the peace your efforts have brought to the
realm, while ever being on the alert to defend it against
all those who might break their pledge and attack it again.

Although it is common enough with many men to act
only when driven by some emotion, so that one may conceive of them as being like incense which smells sweet
only when it is being burned, I cannot help reminding
Your Majesty that such a character trait is dangerous in
any kind of person, and it is particularly so in kings, who
more than all others should be motivated by reason. If
emotion once in a while does in fact bring good results,
it is only a matter of luck, since by its very nature it
misleads men so much that it blinds those who are possessed by it. If a man so deprived of sight occasionally
does find the proper course, it is a marvel if he does not
stray and get lost completely. And if he does not fall
down he will certainly need the best of good fortune
not to falter many times. Often indeed have evils befallen princes and their countries when they have been
more inclined to follow their emotions than their minds,
especially when guided by their whims rather than by

considerations of the public interest. Because of this it is impossible for me not to beg Your Majesty to reflect frequently on this matter in order to confirm more and more in yourself your natural tendency to do the right thing.

I also plead with you to think often of how I have reminded you many times that there is no prince in a worse position than he who, not always able to do those things by himself which it is nevertheless his duty to perform, finds it even harder to let others do them for him. The capability of allowing himself to be served is not one of the least qualities a great king should have. Without this quality, opportunities are often quickly and senselessly lost when favorable action could be taken in settling matters for the advancement of the state.

The late king, your father, being in dire extremity, paid with kind words those who served him, accomplishing with caresses what his lack of funds would not permit him to encourage by other means. Your Majesty is unable to follow the late king in this practice, not being of the same make-up, having instead a natural dryness which you inherited from your mother the Queen, who herself has told you this in my presence several times.[12] I cannot help reminding you that the public interest requires that you treat with consideration those who serve

[12] Louis's father, Henry IV, was a man of great warmth and charm. Louis himself was inclined to be quiet and aloof, except when he lost his temper, which was not infrequently.

you, and at the least it is wise for you to be particularly careful not to say anything that would offend them.

Since I am going to deal later with the subject of the liberality princes should exercise I will say no more about it here, but I will dwell a bit on the bad effects which result from the remarks of those who speak too loosely about their subjects. The blows from a sword are easily healed. But it is not the same with blows of the tongue, especially if they be from the tongue of a king, whose authority renders the pain almost without remedy unless it be provided by the king himself. The higher a stone is thrown, the greater its striking force when it returns. There are many who would give no thought to being cut to pieces by the enemies of their master but who cannot suffer the slightest scratch from his hand. Just as flies do not constitute the diet of the eagle, so the lion is contemptuous of all animals with less than his strength. Likewise a man who attacked a child would be blamed by everyone. In similar fashion, I make bold to say, a great king should never insult his subordinates since they too are relatively weak. History is full of the unfortunate episodes which have resulted from the excessively free rein great men have given to their tongues, causing the unhappiness of those they considered beneath them.

God has seen fit to so endow Your Majesty as to make it natural for you not to do evil, and such being the case, it is only reasonable that you should carefully guard what you say, so that even your words will give no offense.

I am sure, in this matter, that you will not by intent speak offensively, but it is difficult for you not to act impulsively, and sudden waves of emotion occasionally overtake you when you least expect them. I would not be your loyal servant if I did not warn you that both your reputation and your interests require that you have a particular care with regard to them, because such looseness of the tongue, while it may not disturb your conscience, can do much harm to your affairs. Just as to speak well of your enemies is an heroic virtue, so also a prince cannot speak offensively about those who would lay down their lives a thousand times for him and his interests without committing a great fault against the laws of Christianity, to say nothing of those of political wisdom.

A king who has clean hands, a pure heart, and a gentle tongue is not of little virtue, and he who has the first two qualities so eminently as Your Majesty, can with great facility acquire the third. As it is part of the grandeur of kings to be so reserved in their speech that nothing comes out of their mouths which could give offense to their subordinates, so too is it prudent to say nothing derogatory about the principal governmental agencies. Indeed they should be so spoken of as to give occasion for the belief they are held in high regard. The most important undertakings of state so frequently require that they be thwarted that prudence itself indicates they should be pampered in lesser matters.

It is not enough for great princes to resolve never to speak evil of anyone. Good sense requires that they also close their ears to slander and false information, pursuing and even banishing the authors as most dangerous plagues, often capable of poisoning the hearts of princes, as well as the minds of all those who approach them. All those who have free access to the ears of kings, without meriting it, are dangerous, and those who possess their hearts out of pure favoritism are even more so, for in order to preserve such a great treasure it is necessary to have recourse to artifice and malice, in default of the true virtues which invariably are lacking in such people.

I am compelled to say further in this matter that I have always been more apprehensive about the power of such influences over Your Majesty than of the world's greatest kings, and you have more need to guard yourself from the artifice of a valet who wants to take you by surprise than of all the factions the high nobles might form within your realm, even if they should have a common goal. When I first entered your service I learned that those who previously had the honor of serving you were absolutely convinced that you were easily persuaded to suspect them, and having such a conviction their principal care was ever to keep their agents close to you to counteract the suspected evil. The fact of the firmness of Your Majesty in supporting me obliges me to recognize either that this judgment was without foundation or else that mature reflection has erased your youthful weakness. Even so, I cannot help beseeching you to strengthen this trait in your character so that the attitude you have been pleased to take toward me will be the one naturally expected by anyone who may succeed me. In addition I must also say to you that just as the ears of princes ought to be closed to calumny, so also should they be open to all truths useful to the state, and in like manner just as their tongues should never give utterance to words prejudicial to the reputation of others, so they should be able to speak freely and boldly when questions of public interest are at stake.

I mention these two points because I have often observed that it is irksome to Your Majesty to be patient enough to listen to what is even of the greatest importance to you, and that when the proper prosecution of your affairs requires you to make your will known, not only in cases involving the great nobles but even in those concerned with men of little or no consequence, you have great difficulty in coming to a decision, if you foresee that it will not be pleasing to those affected. I acknowledge that this apprehensiveness is evidence of your goodness, but I would be guilty of flattery if I did not say that it also is the effect of a kind of weakness which although tolerable in a private individual, is hardly so in a great king because of the difficulties which can arise from it.

I make no point of the fact that public knowledge of such indecision might throw the blame and anger aroused

by specific acts upon Your Majesty's council, because
this would be a small price to pay for the proper advancement of public business. What needs to be considered,
however, is that it often happens that whatever may be
the authority of a minister it is not great enough to produce the desired results, for which the immediate voice
of a sovereign with absolute power is required. Besides,
if certain of the great nobles succeed in persuading themselves that a bad conscience prevents the king from ex-
ercising the powers of his office with absolute authority,
they will always try by importunity to reverse the suggestions of sound reason, until in the end their audacity
can reach the point where, knowing the hesitancy of
their prince to play the part of master, they in turn get
bored with playing the part of subject.

It is necessary to have the masculine virtue of making
decisions rationally, rather than to slide down the easy
slope of inclination, which often leads princes over great
precipices. If inclination, covering their eyes, leads them
to do blindly whatever pleases them, it can produce great
evil if they follow it with too little moderation. On the
other hand, the natural aversions of princes, often without explanation, can cause even greater difficulties if
reason does not provide the requisite tempering. Whatever the occasion may be, Your Majesty has need of your
gift of prudence to balance your leaning toward these
two tendencies. But you need to balance your leaning
toward the latter even more than toward the former,

since it is easier to do harm in following your aversions, which requires nothing of a king but a command, while for him to do good in accordance with his inclinations can be accomplished only with some sacrifice on his part, something many people find hard to do.

These two lines of action are both contrary to the outlook of kings, especially if, given to little reflection on such matters, they are generally inclined to follow emotion rather than reason. As a result they are sometimes led to involvement in the private quarrels which only too frequently occur at their courts, from which I have seen great misfortunes arise. Dignity, however, requires them to keep to the path of reason, which represents the only cause they should espouse. Under no circumstances can they do otherwise without stripping themselves of the qualification of judge and sovereign, for by joining sides they thereby lower themselves, in some degree, toward the level of their subjects. By following such a course they expose their states to the many cabals and factions which as a result spring up. Those who wish to circumvent the power of a king and know so well they can accomplish nothing by force, give countenance only to the use of intrigue, artifice, and plotting, which needless to say are the cause of much trouble to governments.

The absolute sincerity a man making his testament ought to employ does not permit me to finish this section without making a confession as true as it is advantageous to Your Majesty's glory. It is to bear witness to everyone that the law of God has always been the barrier capable of checking whatever impulse toward violence coming from either inclination or aversion might attempt to overwhelm you. Subject as you are to these lesser faults of mankind, you are exempt, by the grace of God, from the most conspicuous imperfections of princes.

CHAPTER VII

THE REFORMATION
OF THE ROYAL
HOUSEHOLD

The acquisition of useful techniques and sound discipline always begins with the mastery of simple undertakings. On that basis, the first thing an architect does when he plans to build a great edifice is to make a model of it, in which the details are so readily observable that they accurately serve him in drafting the final plan. If he has any insurmountable difficulty at this stage he rejects his original concept, common sense indicating to even the slowest mind that what is impossible in the model is even more so in the ultimate undertaking. In like manner, even those of little intelligence know that just as the nature of man is an analogue of the world at large, so are private families the true models of republics and states, and everyone holds for certain that he who cannot or will not manage his family is hardly capable of running a state. It is for this reason that in order to succeed in prescribing for the reformation of this realm I should commence with that of Your Majesty's household.

I confess, however, that I have never heretofore dared to undertake it, because the goodness of Your Majesty having always been averse to giving orders which you deemed of little consequence whenever they have dealt only with individuals, one could not propose such a plan without openly shocking your inclination. I was also restrained by the knowledge of the fact that many men, close to you in the greatest familiarity, could have shunted to one side those orders most necessary to your state as a prelude to disposing of those aimed at reforming your household, the renovation of which would be disadvantageous to them. But many a testament brings to light numerous intentions which the testator had not dared to divulge during his lifetime, and this one will beseech Your Majesty to undertake the reformation of your household. So far the task has been avoided, partly because it seemed outwardly more easy to reform than the state, although in truth it was more difficult, and partly because wisdom obliges us, in certain instances, to suffer little disadvantages in order to preclude greater ones.

While everyone knows there has never been a king who has advanced the prestige of his state as much as Your Majesty has, it also cannot be denied that no one has ever allowed the reputation of his household to sink so low. Foreigners who have visited France in my time

have often been astounded to see a state so grand combined with a household so mean. It has declined, even if
gradually and imperceptibly, to the point where there
are persons possessing responsibilities of the highest order
who during the reign of your predecessors would not
have dared to aspire to the lowest; everything is in confusion from the kitchen to your private quarters.

In place of the arrangements which prevailed in the
time of the king your father, when the officers of the
crown and the great nobles of the realm ordinarily ate
in the royal dining room, now in your day it appears as
if it were filled by valets and men of the lowest aristo-
cratic rank. Indeed these opportunities have come to
mean so little that sometimes they are despised, rather
than sought after eagerly. Foreigners have often criticized even your personal table, noting that you are
served by common and dirty scullions in place of the
gentlemen who customarily serve other kings.

I well know that this practice was not introduced in
your time. But being ancient does not make it the more
tolerable, particularly since it detracts from the dignity
and grandeur of so great a prince. I am also conversant
with the fact that this practice has been suffered up to
now under the pretext of the king's safety, since it is
impossible to hold courtiers responsible for an untoward
event if they themselves have neither touched nor seen
what is borne to Your Majesty. But this reasoning seems
ridiculous to me, there being little likelihood that a scul-

lion would be more faithful to his master than a gentleman would be. The latter could, after all, easily betray him on many other occasions if he so desired. Eighty young gentlemen, whom Your Majesty supports as pages either in your chamber or in your stables, would be much better employed at this service, instead of grudgingly serving your first gentlemen or equerries who order them around. They would then be serving the one who pays them, and having more dignified positions they would acquit themselves with greater fidelity.

Cleanliness, a pleasing practice anywhere, is even more desirable as an attribute of the household of a king. Opulence in furnishings is much more necessary there because foreigners recognize the grandeur of princes only by appearances. But although Your Majesty is richly endowed with beautiful items, they are allowed to deteriorate instead of being preserved. One often has seen in your chambers things which, when you are ready to dispose of them, even those to whom they have been passed have not wished to make use of any longer.

Entry into your private quarters has been granted to everyone, not only to the prejudice of your dignity but also, which is even more important, to the endangering of your personal safety. While in audience with you ambassadors have often found themselves more jostled by footmen, pages, and other lesser officers than by the great aristocrats of your state. And yet your dignity and the ancient custom of the realm demand that upon such occasions Your Majesty be accompanied by princes, dukes, peers, officers of the crown, and other dignitaries of your government. I know that different countries have different customs, that in Spain the great nobles rarely see their king, that in England custom is so well established in this matter that although all doors are open, one sees in the bedrooms and private quarters of the king only those whose entry is sanctioned by their rank or their office. I also know it is a privilege of those who wear your crown to be surrounded by their subjects, but distinctions should be drawn so that ordinarily it is confined to your nobility to whom, on the occasions of receiving foreigners, only a limited number of qualified persons of lesser station might be added, all with the aim of emphasizing the grandeur and significance of this prerogative. In a word, disorder is so universal in the entire household of Your Majesty that not even the slightest function is exempt from it.

Although all great princes go to considerable pains to be well supplied with horses befitting their station, Your Majesty has never had any in your great stables truly suitable for public display, although more money has been spent on them than under any of your predecessors. It would be easy for me to specify many other defects no less conspicuous than this, but I will not enter into details of so widespread a confusion, both because it would be too difficult to do so without sinking below the dignified level which such a body of recommendations as this one should have, and because it is not necessary to proclaim an evil publicly in order to recognize it and prescribe for its remedy. I shall be carrying out my task if I can suggest to Your Majesty the proper way to bring as much luster to your household as there now is slovenliness and disorder.

The first prerequisite necessary to such an end is that Your Majesty must really want this reformation, for it is certain in matters of this nature that the will of kings, like that of God in cosmic affairs, makes the same thing out of wishing and fulfilling. The second is that in the future it should be your pleasure to fill the most important offices of your household only with persons of high birth who have all the requisite qualifications for the dignified performance of their duties. No matter how noble a given officeholder may be, he will apply himself to even the smallest undertakings to the utmost of his ability, because he will be aware of the ultimate consequences they actually have.

Unless the stewards, for example, are particularly careful to have the dining rooms cleaned as soon as the tables are cleared, both morning and evening, they will be failing at one of the basic responsibilities of their office. Much the same thing can be said about all of the principal officers, especially of the first gentlemen of the chamber, who ought to see to it that the apartments of Your Majesty are kept clean and in good order. In this regard it would not be too much to clean up and scent the rooms five or six times a day, because of the great crowd of people inevitably there, no matter how efficiently your schedule is managed. If each holder of each position is adequate to his function everything in Your Majesty's household will go as you wish it, and on this one formula rests the proper management of the remainder of your affairs. For, whatever regulation one might establish, it will be absolutely useless if there are no men capable of making it observed, but if there are, they will be intelligent enough to carry out what common sense indicates to be proper to both the dignity of their office and the service of their master.

The third consists in that Your Majesty should in the future be served in all your household offices, except the lowest, by gentlemen. This will, in addition to contributing a great deal to your dignity, make the nobility all the more devoted to you, seeing that they can advance themselves by serving your person. By such a policy Your Majesty could make the four companies of men at arms the four best in the realm, for it is certain that more than enough gentlemen would be eager to be members of such a body, provided they are freely given the positions which now are sold at auction to the highest bidder.

Under this arrangement such men would be glad to hold these positions as could not be prevailed upon now when they are monopolized by unworthy people. And all would willingly take them for the access it would give them to court, where good luck and proximity could

advance their fortunes at any moment. Still another benefit could come to you from this reform in that it would
decrease the number of middle class men exempted from
the *taille* [13] by virtue of holding a position in your household, thereby increasing the ranks of those who help the
common people bear the burden by which they are now
borne down.

The fourth is that Your Majesty should in the future
grant all positions in your household without charge,
never permitting them to be sold under any circumstances whatsoever. It may be said, perhaps, that it is un-
fair that those who buy offices be deprived of the right
to sell them. But if it is impossible to make reforms of
great public usefulness except at the expense of private
individuals, the expense is a minor matter, especially
since not having bought their offices with the assurance
of the right of resale, as is the case with those offices sold
in the provision for an annual payment to the crown, [14]
one can deprive them of the hope, which they have in-
vented for themselves, without committing a wrong.

And although some private individuals might be in-
jured by such a reform, all of the nobility and other

[13] See note 6, p. 32.

[14] It was principally by this device, known as the *parquet*, that
the temporary patents of nobility attached to certain administrative
posts had been made heritable. This was the channel through
which the so-called nobility of the robe emerged. Whenever Richelieu uses the word nobility, however, he is referring to the old-
line "true" nobility of the sword.

important personages would find it most advantageous. In place of the former arrangement, under which they had to sell a good part of their patrimony in order to acquire an office, something that often ruined the best families in the realm, they would henceforth have to count on their merit. This would at one and the same time prevent the loss of their wealth and oblige them to acquire attractive virtues, which in the present century have become too much despised, all things now having their price. Besides, there are so many ways for taking care of those who for special reasons should be considered as exceptions to the rule that the public will receive the benefit of their talents, which Your Majesty will have procured, while worthy lesser individuals, who could otherwise justly complain, will receive no injury.

It is impossible to doubt the usefulness of these proposals, and the ease with which they can be executed is manifest, since, as I have said above, the firmness and constancy of your will is all that is necessary to bring about the reëstablishment of your house in all its original splendor.

CHAPTER VIII

THE QUALIFICATIONS FOR

ROYAL COUNCILLORS

It is an important question among political thinkers which is to be desired, a prince who governs solely on his own initiative or one who, less sure of his superior abilities, defers to his council and acts only on advice. One could write complete books on all the arguments which have been advanced on both sides of this question, but to get to the subject directly as it is raised here, the prince who is guided by his council, rather than his own ideas alone, is to be preferred to the one who believes his own head superior to those of his councillors. Indeed I can only say that the worst government is that which has no other guiding force than the will of an incompetent and presumptuous king who ignores his council, while the best of all is that one whose moving principle is embodied in the mind of the monarch who, although capable of acting by himself, has so much modesty and soundness of judgment that he acts only after seeking sound advice, on the theory that one eye cannot see as clearly as several.

.   .   .   .

A capable prince is a great treasure to a state. An able council which functions smoothly is no less important. The two working in concert are of priceless value, since from this comes the well-being of the state. It is certain that the happiest states are those having the wisest princes and councillors.

.   .   .   .

The qualifications for a councillor do not include that of a pedantic mind. There is nothing more dangerous for the state than those who wish to govern by maxims they have learned from books. They do, indeed, often ruin countries this way, for the past has little bearing on the present, when the nature of conditions, places, and people is different. The councillors require only goodness and firmness of mind, stable judgment (true source of wisdom), a reasonable acquaintance with literature, a general knowledge of history and of the organization of existing states around the world, especially including the home country.

.   .   .   .

Presumption is one of the greatest vices a man in public office can have and if humility is not required of those charged with the direction of state, certainly modesty is. Indeed, often greater minds are less capable of easy association with others, and the lack of such a quality more than outweighs their numerous virtues and renders them unfit for governing. Without modesty such men are so enamored of their own opinions that they condemn all others even if they are better, and the conceit of their personal make-up, combined with the authority at their disposal, makes them completely intolerable.

The ablest man in the world should often listen to the advice of even those he considers less able than himself. While it is the essence of wisdom on the part of a minister of state to speak little, it is also wise to listen a great deal. One can draw profit from all kinds of suggestions; those which are good carry their own justifications, and the bad ones confirm the good.

. . . .

These remarks will present to posterity a proof of my integrity, for they prescribe qualities I have not always myself been able to emulate. I have, however, always dealt civilly with those on public business. The nature of government affairs naturally requires one to refuse the requests of many men, but this does not permit a person to accompany his decisions with unpleasant words or facial expressions. My poor health, however, has not made it possible for me to see every suppliant, as I would have wished, and this has so often troubled me that I have several times given serious thought to resigning. Nevertheless, I can truthfully say that a careful management of what little strength I have has made it possible for me to fulfill my duty to the state, even if I have been unable to satisfy everyone.

·   ·   ·   ·   ·   ·   ·   ·

Probity and courage give birth to a boldness honest enough to tell kings what is useful for them, even if such information is not always agreeable to them. I say an honest boldness, because if it is not kept well in hand and always respectful it becomes not one of the leading virtues of a councillor of state but one of the principal vices. It is necessary to speak to kings with words of silk. It is the duty of a faithful councillor to inform them privately and cautiously of their faults, but it is a grave error to do so publicly. To speak aloud something which ought to be whispered in the ear is a slight which can be criminal in him from whom it comes if he advertises the weaknesses of his prince to his own intended gain, that is, if he cares more, through vain ostentation, to expose what he disapproves of than to bring about its genuine correction. Courage and sustained attention give such a solidity to plans conceived by a sound mind and pursued with firm determination that they may be put into operation smoothly without the fluctuations so often produced by the irresponsibility of the French.

I have not mentioned the physical strength and good health required of a minister of state because while they are a great boon when combined with all the intellectual attributes mentioned above, they are not so necessary to councillors as to be indispensable. There are many positions in the state for which they are absolutely necessary because these call for physical as well as mental energy, in particular to move about quickly from place to place. But he who holds the helm of state and is responsible only for the general direction of affairs does not need so strong a physique. Just as the movement of the heavenly bodies requires a guiding intelligence, so intellectual force is alone sufficient for the management of the state; strength of limb plays no part in such matters.[15]

.   .   .   .

After having examined and recognized the qualifications desirable in those to be employed as ministers of state I should also say that just as too many doctors sometimes bring on the death rather than the cure of an ill person, so too does the state often receive more harm than benefit if the number of councillors be too great. I must add specifically that good results cannot be brought about if there are more than four, and even more emphatically it is necessary that one among them have superior authority, being like the prime mover, directing others while he himself is directed only by his own mind.[16]

.   .   .   .

[15] Richelieu is here speaking in his own defense.
[16] This introduces the concept of a prime minister.

Your Majesty having chosen your councillors, it is your obligation to see to it that they can work for the grandeur and felicity of your realm.[17] Four main things are requisite to this end.

The first is that Your Majesty have confidence in them and that they be aware of it. This is absolutely necessary because otherwise even the best councillors can feel they are suspected by their princes, and if ministers are not sure their fidelity is known they may restrain themselves on many occasions when their silence is quite damaging.

. . . .

The second is to require them to speak freely and assure them they can do so without peril.

. . . .

The third is to reward them liberally so that they will believe that their services will not be without adequate recompense. This is especially necessary because there are few men who love virtue naked.

. . . .

The fourth is to empower and support them so openly that they are assured of no need of fearing either the artifices or the power of those who would try to destroy

---

[17] From this point to the end of the chapter Richelieu in describing the ideal relationship is picturing as well his own hopes and apprehensions, and hence himself.

them. The interest of the prince obliges him to do this, since no man can serve the public without attracting the hate and the envy of everyone, and there are few selfless enough to perform well if they fear the result to be personally hazardous.

. . . .

In order to avoid all embarrassment and to guard against the plots which evildoers can think up to destroy the best of men, as well as not to be deprived of the means of discovering the underhanded activities of those who serve such ends, the prince should consider as calumny all that which is only whispered to him and so refuse to listen to it. If, on the other hand, someone wishes to maintain what he has to say in the presence of those he accuses, then he should be listened to, with a promise of ample reward if he says something of provable importance to the public good, and a similar assurance of severe punishment if his accusation is false, or of minor significance even if true.

. . . .

PART II

CHAPTER I

THE REIGN OF GOD THE

FIRST ESSENTIAL

The reign of God is the principle basic to the good government of states, and is, in fact, so absolutely necessary that without this foundation no prince can rule well nor can any state be happy and successful. It would be easy to write entire books on a subject so important for which the Bible, the Fathers, and all manner of histories provide us with an infinite number of precepts, examples, and exhortations aimed toward the same end. But this is a thing so well known to everyone with common sense that to say to a person that he was not created spontaneously but rather that he has a God for a Creator and hence a Director is a common truth which nature has already implanted in his heart with indelible characters. So many princes have blackened their reigns and ruined their countries by basing their conduct on a course of action contrary to their better judgment, and so many have been overwhelmed with blessings for having sub-

mitted their authority to Him whence it came, for having looked for their own glory only in that of their Creator, and for having had more concern for His reign than
for their own, that I will dwell no longer on a truth too
self-evident to need any proof.

I will say one thing only. Just as it is impossible for the
reign of a prince who leaves vice and disorder unbridled
to be happy, so also will God not willingly suffer to be
unhappy him who takes particular care to establish his
empire within the boundaries of His kingdom. Nothing
is more influential for the well-being of the social order
than the public life of princes, which is the living law
speaking and ruling with more efficacy than all those
edicts which might be promulgated to make people seek
the good ends desired. It is true that whatever evil practices a sovereign may adopt, he sins more by the bad example he sets than by the nature of his actual misdeed
itself. It is also undeniable that whatever law he may pro-
mulgate if he practices what he prescribes, his example is
no less useful to the enforcement of his wishes than all
the penalties of his ordinances, no matter how potent
they seem. The good conduct of a moral prince banishes
more vice from his realm than all the orders he can give
looking toward the desired end.

The prudence and rectitude of him who does not
swear will soon put an end to oaths and blasphemies, only
too common in governing circles. This is more important
than whatever discipline can be brought to bear on those

who abandon themselves to such execrable practices. All of this is not to say that one should abstain from rigorously punishing scandalous conduct, swearing and blasphemy. Indeed, this is something about which it is impossible to be too demanding, and, no matter how saintly and exemplary the life of a prince or magistrate may be, he will never be considered as having done what was expected of him if, in addition to encouraging people to follow him by his example, he does not constrain them to do so by enacting rigorous laws.

There is not a single sovereign in the world who is not obliged by this principle to procure the conversion of those who, living within his kingdom, have deviated from the path to salvation. But as man is reasonable enough by nature to find his way ultimately to so good an end, prudence does not permit anything so hazardous as to risk uprooting the grain while pulling out the tares, for it would be difficult to purge the state in any but a gentle way without a shock capable of bringing down ruin upon it, or at the very least greatly weakening it.[18]

Since princes are expected to establish God's true church, they should be very thorough in banishing all

---

[18] This is the famous passage in which Richelieu states his case for the toleration of the Huguenots, whose religious privileges he did not think it expedient to touch although he had already stripped them of the political powers they had won in the Edict of Nantes in 1598. The next paragraph, however, indicates that his tolerance was not a passive one, and is of a piece with his lifelong support of militant missionary work among the French Protestants.

false imitations of it, which are so dangerous to the state that one may say with complete truth that this kind of hypocrisy has always been used to clothe the enormity of the most pernicious undertakings. Many people, who are as weak as they are malicious, sometimes use this as a kind of ruse. Particularly is this the case in approaching women, since their sex is more given to transports of devotion which is, however, of so little depth that they are vulnerable to such stratagems, as they depend less on real substance than upon cunning.

CHAPTER II

REASON SHOULD GUIDE

THE GOVERNING OF

A STATE

Common sense leads each one of us to understand that man, having been endowed with reason, should do nothing except that which is reasonable, since otherwise he would be acting contrary to his nature, and by consequence contrary to Him Who is its Creator. It further teaches us that the more a man is great and conspicuous, the more he ought to be conscious of this principle and the less he ought to abuse the rational process which constitutes his being, because the ascendency he has over other men requires him to preserve that part of his nature and his purpose which was specifically given to him by Him Who chose him for elevation.

From these two principles it clearly follows that if man is sovereignly reasonable he ought to make reason sovereign, which requires not only that he do nothing not in conformity with it, but also that he make all those who are under his authority reverence it and follow it religiously. This precept is the source of another, which teaches us that since we should never want the accomplishment of anything not reasonable and just, neither should we ever want the accomplishment of anything without having it carried out and our commands followed by complete obedience, because otherwise reason would not really reign sovereign. The practice of this rule is quite easy because love is a most powerful motive in winning obedience, and it is impossible for subjects not to love a prince if they know that reason is the guide of all his actions. Authority constrains obedience, but reason captivates it. It is much more expedient to lead men by means which imperceptibly win their wills than, as is more the practice, by those which coerce them.

If it is true that reason ought to be the torch which lights the conduct of both princes and their states, it is also true that there is nothing in nature less compatible with reason than emotion. It can so blind a person that it makes the shadow seem like the substance, and a prince must above all avoid acting upon such a basis. It would make him doubly odious, since it is directly contrary to what distinguishes man from the animals. One often has to repent at leisure what emotion has hastily engendered, but such results never occur when action springs from reasonable consideration. It is for such reasons necessary to back one's decision with a firm will, because this is the only way to make oneself obeyed, and just as humility is the first foundation of Christian perfection, so

obedience is the most important part of the subjection
so necessary to the well-being of states, which, if it is
defective, cannot flourish.

There are many things which by their very nature are
difficult neither to order nor to carry out, but it is necessary to will them efficaciously, that is to say, with complete firmness and lasting attention, and so that after the
execution has been ordered, severe punishment falls on
any who disobey. Those tasks which appear the most
difficult, even almost impossible, seem so only because
of the lack of determination with which we view them
and command their execution. And it is true that subjects will always religiously obey when princes are firm
and relentless in their commands, from which it follows
that if states are poorly governed princes are all the more
responsible for it, since it is certain that their weakness
and indifference are the cause of it. In a word, just as
to will firmly and to do what one wills are the same thing
in a true prince, so too to will weakly or not to will at
all are alike in the opposite sense in that nothing is ever
accomplished.

The government of kingdoms requires a manly bearing and an inflexible will, contrary to indecision which
exposes those who are its victims to the schemes of their
enemies. It is necessary, in all cases, to act with vigor,
principally because even if the outcome of an undertaking is not good, at least we can know that having omitted
nothing which could have made it succeed we can spare

ourselves the shame of responsibility although we cannot avoid the evil of a real misfortune. Even when one fails in honestly trying to do his duty the disgrace should make him happy, while contrariwise, if success comes to him accidentally when not abiding by what he is obligated to by honor and conscience, he should be considered most unfortunate since he can draw no satisfaction from it equal to the real losses arising from the knowledge of the means he has employed. In the past the larger part of the great plans drafted for France have come to naught because the first serious obstacle confronting them has been sufficient to cause an end of effort on the part of those who in all justice should have carried them through, and if things have resulted differently during the reign of Your Majesty it is because of the perseverance with which matters have constantly been pursued.

If, at a given time, it seems inexpedient to attempt to carry out a particular plan, one should postpone action and turn to something else, and if this is also interrupted good sense indicates we should again take up the first project as soon as the time and circumstances are favorable. In a word, nothing ought to be allowed to turn us permanently away from a good objective unless some untoward accident makes it entirely unachievable, and we must never fail to do whatever is necessary to bring about the execution of that which we have rightly resolved to accomplish.

It is this which obliges me to speak here of secrecy and diligence, both of which are so necessary to the success of affairs as to dwarf all other attributes. Both experience and reason make it evident that what is suddenly presented ordinarily astonishes in such a fashion as to deprive one of the means of opposing it, while if the execution of a plan is undertaken slowly the gradual revelation of it can create the impression that it is only being projected and will not necessarily be executed. From this it follows that women, by nature indolent and unable to keep secrets, are little suited to government, particularly if one also considers that they are subject to their emotions and consequently little susceptible to reason and justice, attributes which should exclude them from all public office. This is not to say that a few might be found so free of these faults as to make them admissible to public service. There are few general rules for which no exceptions can be found. This era itself bears witness to several women whose deeds cannot be praised enough. But it is true that their weakness denies them the masculine vigor necessary to public administration, and it is almost impossible for them to govern without a base exploitation of their sex, or without acts of injustice and cruelty arising from the disorderly ascendency of their emotions.

CHAPTER III

PUBLIC INTEREST THE

FIRST OBJECTIVE

The public interest ought to be the sole objective of the prince and his councillors, or, at the least, both are obliged to have it foremost in mind, and preferred to all private gain. It is impossible to overestimate the good which a prince and those serving him in government can do if they religiously follow this principle, and one can hardly imagine the evils which befall a state if private interest is preferred to the public good and actually gains the ascendency. True philosophy, as well as the precepts of both Christianity and sound politics, teach this truth so clearly that a prince's councillors can hardly too often remind him of so necessary a principle, nor the prince punish too severely those members of his council despicable enough not to practice it.

I cannot but remark in this regard that the prosperity which has invariably blessed Spain for several centuries is solely due to the fact that its council has given prefer-ence to the public interest above all other interests, while most of the misfortunes which have befallen France have occurred because many of those employed in government administration have been more concerned with their own advancement than with that of the public welfare. The former has always pursued the public interest, which by its very nature has induced it to act in the fashion most advantageous to the state, while the latter, accommodating everything to their selfish profit or whims, have often twisted the execution of government programs in order to make them privately more agreeable or advantageous. Neither death nor the changing of ministers has ever brought any modification in the council's program in Spain. But it has not been the same in this kingdom, where policy has been changed in more ways than simply by a change in councillors. It has even taken such a variety of directions under the same councillors because of the diversity of their advice that this assuredly would have ruined the monarchy if God in His goodness had not found in the imperfections of our nation the necessary defenses against the attendant evils.

If the complexity of our interests and our natural inconstancy often carry us close to dangerous precipices, our irresponsibility itself does not long permit us to remain firm and stable even in what is for our own good, and we switch about so quickly that our enemies, being unable to adopt feasible programs to cope with such frequent fluctuations, are unable to profit from our faults.

Your own particular council having some time ago altered this mode of conduct, the course of your affairs has also changed, to the great benefit of your realm, and if, in the future, the example of the reign of Your Majesty is followed, your neighbors will never again have the advantages they formerly enjoyed. But this realm, displaying the same wisdom as prevails in theirs, will doubtless share the same good fortune, for although to be wise and to be happy are not always the same thing, nevertheless the best policy to adopt in the hope of avoiding unhappiness is to follow the path indicated by prudence and reason, and not to proceed in the aimless way customary with most men, especially the French.

If those in whose hands Your Majesty places the direction of your affairs have the ability and the probity of which I have spoken above, you have no more worries in this regard, which of itself offers no problems since the concern for the prince's own reputation and the public interest have a common end.

Princes ordinarily easily consent to the over-all plans proposed for their states because in so doing they have nothing in mind save reason and justice, which they easily accept when they meet no obstacle which turns them off the path. When the occasion arises, however, of putting into practical action the wise programs they have adopted, they do not always show the same firmness. Distracting interests, pity and compassion, favoritism and importunities of all sorts obstruct their best intentions to a degree they often cannot overcome sufficiently to ignore private consideration, which ought never influence public affairs. It is in such matters that they should summon up all their strength against inclinations toward weakness, keeping before their eyes the fact that those whom God has destined to protect others should have no characteristics but those advantageous to the public interest, and to which they should adhere inflexibly.

CHAPTER IV

FORESIGHT NECESSARY TO

GOOD GOVERNMENT

Nothing is more necessary in governing a state than foresight, since by its use one can easily prevent many evils which can be corrected only with great difficulty if allowed to transpire. Just as a doctor who knows how to prevent illness is more esteemed than the one who works cures, so too should ministers of state always remind both themselves and their masters that it is more important to anticipate the future than to dwell upon the present, since with enemies of the state, as with diseases, it is better to advance to the attack than to wait and drive them out after they have invaded.

Those who follow any other procedure will encounter great difficulties, for which it will be unusually hard to find subsequent remedies. However, it is quite usual for ordinary men to content themselves with little effort, preferring to enjoy the pleasures of a month rather than demand of themselves a few days of effort which could guarantee many trouble-free years, a matter they ignore, for they see only the present and cannot mold the future by a wise foresight. Those who live only from day to day live happily for themselves; but those who are subject to their rule live unhappily. On the other hand, men who see far ahead do nothing precipitously, since they consider things well in advance and it is more difficult to make a mistake when something has been thought through. There are occasions, to be sure, when it is not possible to deliberate at length because the nature of the matter does not permit it. But in affairs not of this kind it is best to sleep on them, making up with the speed of final execution for any delay created during their thorough consideration.

There was a time when no orders were given in this realm with a view to anticipating problems, and when even after the evil results occurred only palliative remedies were applied, because it was impossible to be thorough without injuring many close at hand. Private interest was then preferred to public interest, and because of this one had to reconcile oneself to the open wounds instead of healing them, which only multiplied the evils in the realm. For some years now, thanks be to God, there has been a change in this way of doing things, with a success so happy that beyond convincing us by its reasonableness we are obliged by the great results achieved to adhere to it even more firmly.

It is necessary to sleep like the lion, without closing

one's eyes, so that one may instantly ward off the slightest misfortune which may arise, and remembering that
just as consumption does not affect the pulse even though
it is fatal, so it is often the case with states that the evils
which are imperceptible at the time of their origin and
of which we are little aware are the most dangerous and
finally become of greatest consequence. The extraordinary care it is necessary to take in order not to be sur-
prised on such occasions goes far to explain why those
states governed by wise men are generally happy. In
like fashion it is easy to foresee that those which are governed less wisely are bound to be far less happy.

The abler a man is the more aware he is of the governmental responsibilities with which he is charged. Public
administration so completely occupies the best minds in
its service that the uninterrupted attention they are obligated to give government matters in order to foresee evils
which might arise deprives them of all repose and relax-
ation. Their principal compensation can come from seeing many other men sleep without fear in the shadow of
their protection and thus live happily as a result of their
misery.[19]

It is necessary to see as far in advance as possible what
will be the outcome of one's acts in order to avoid self-
deception, but the wisdom and vision of men have defi-
nite limits beyond which they can see nothing, God
alone being able to see the final objective of things. It

[19] Richelieu is obviously thinking of himself here.

suffices often to know that projects which one under-takes are just and possible in order to embark upon them with good reason. God concurs with all the good deeds of men by a general coöperation, which serves their ends, and it is incumbent upon them to use in all their under-takings the freedom of mind which divine wisdom has made them capable of employing prudently. When, therefore, they are involved in important matters con-cerning the governing of men, after having satisfied the obligation which they have of opening wide their eyes to take more adequate measures, after having weighed every consideration of which the human mind is capable, they should rely upon the goodness of God, Who, some-times inspiring men with that which has all eternity as its objective, leads them by the hand toward that goal.

CHAPTER V

THE USES OF PUNISHMENTS

AND REWARDS

It is a common but nevertheless true saying which has long been repeated by intelligent men that punishments and rewards are the two most important instruments of government in a realm. It is certain that, whatever else one may do in governing states, one must be inflexible in punishing those who fail to obey, and religiously scrupulous in rewarding those who perform notable services. In other words, one would not govern badly if guided by this precept since most people can be held to their duty through either fear or hope. I rate punishments, I must say, higher than rewards, because if it were necessary to dispense with one of these, it would be better to give up the latter than the former. The good ought to be adhered to for its own sake, and in all justice no one should be rewarded for this. But there is no crime which does not violate those precepts men are obligated to obey, so that the punishment to be

expected for disobedience of this sort is therefore justi-
fied, and this obligation is so direct in many cases that to
let the act go unpunished is to commit a further error.[20]

I speak here of things which injure the state and which
have been premeditated, and not of those lesser offenses
which result from chance or misfortune, toward which
princes may and should often show indulgence. But
while in matters of this sort it can be praiseworthy to
pardon, it is a criminal omission not to punish breaches
which open the door to licentious abandon. Both theologians and political experts agree that on special occasions it would be an error not to pardon certain individuals, but it would be inexcusable for those charged with
public responsibilities to substitute indulgence for severe
punishment. Experience teaches those who have had
long practice in this world that men easily lose the memory of rewards and, when they are heaped with them,
they expect even more, and become both ambitious and
ungrateful at the same time. This teaches us to realize
that punishments are a surer means of holding a person
to his duty, since people are less likely to forget what has
made an impression on their emotions. This is more persuasive for most men than reason, which has little power
over many minds.

To be severe in dealing with private individuals who
glory in disobeying the laws and orders of the state makes
a good impression on the people, and one can commit no

[20] Here Richelieu is describing one of his basic views.

greater crime against the public interest than to be indulgent toward those who violate them. In thinking over
the many cabals, factions, and plottings which have occurred in this realm in my time, I can recall none in
which leniency induced any person with evil inclinations
to rectify the error of his ways. All ordinarily returned
to their mischief, usually with greater effect the second
time than the first, because they had become more cunning. The indulgence practiced hitherto in this realm
often created extensive and deplorable difficulties. Misdeeds going unpunished, each official exploited his office,
and without the slightest regard for the responsibilities
of his function he only considered what further profit
he might derive from it for himself.

If the men of old thought that it was dangerous to live
under a prince who was relentless in enforcing the law,
they also noted that it was even worse to live in a state
where indulgence opened the door to all sorts of license.
Any prince or magistrate who fears that he will exercise
too great a rigor should hold himself accountable to God
and worry about the censure of wise men only if he fails
to do what the law prescribes. I have often pressed upon
Your Majesty, and I beseech you again now, to remember that although there are many princes who need to be
dissuaded from severity in order to prevent unnecessary
cruelty, in Your Majesty's case the need is rather to be
diverted from an unfounded clemency. The latter is
more dangerous than cruelty even, since leniency gives

rise to the ultimately necessary exercise of a degree of cruelty which could have been avoided by the employment of an efficacious punishment at an earlier time.

The rod, which is the symbol of justice, ought never to be idle. I also appreciate that it should not be so rigorously employed as to make the wielder appear to be destitute of all mercy. But this latter quality should never be carried to the point of indulgence toward disorders which, however small they may at first be, can often become so prejudicial to the welfare of the state as to cause its ruin. If there is anyone in this realm so poorly advised as to condemn the severity necessary in public affairs on the basis that up to the present it has not been utilized, it is only necessary to open his eyes for him. He will see what leniency, heretofore only too common, and the sole cause of the failure to observe law and order, can produce. Indeed, the continued effects still require utilization of the direst remedies in order to check their course. Many of the plots against kings in the past have had no source other than the too great indulgence with which they were handled. In fact, those who know our history cannot ignore this truth, for which I can produce evidence beyond suspicion because it is drawn from the mouths of our enemies, which under other circumstances would render it suspect.

Cardinal Zapata,[21] a man of keen intellect, on meeting

[21] Antonio Zapata de Mendoza (1550–1635), Cardinal and Archbishop of Toledo, named Grand Inquisitor in 1626.

Barrault [22] and Bautru [23] in the antechamber of his master
the king a quarter of an hour after the arrival in Madrid of
the news of the execution of the Duke of Montmorency,[24] asked them the reason for the conviction of the
Duke. Bautru replied quickly, with his customary certi-
tude, and in Spanish: "His mistakes." "No," said the
Cardinal, "because of the indulgence of former kings,"
which is to say that the crimes committed by earlier rulers
in the form of excessive indulgence were more the cause
of the punishment of the Duke than his own errors.

With regard to crimes of state it is necessary to close
the door to pity, ignoring the pleas of interested individuals and the clamor of an ignorant populace, which occasionally condemns what is most useful and even indispensable to it. Christians ought to forget their personal
injuries, but magistrates must not forget those which affect the public interest.[25] In fact, to leave them unpun-

[22] Antoine de Jaubert, comte de Barrault, French ambassador to
Spain, 1629–34.

[23] Guillaume Bautru, *chargé de mission* at Madrid.

[24] Henri II, duc de Montmorency (1595–1632), Governor of
Languedoc and Marshal, head of one of the greatest noble houses
and a popular idol. Drawn by the scheming brother of Louis XIII,
Gaston, duc d'Orléans, into open rebellion against Richelieu, he
was defeated, tried, and executed. It was a culminating crisis in the
cardinal's struggle with the aristocracy, which for the most part
henceforth stood in awe of him. There is, therefore, much reason
to refresh the king's memory at this point in the Testament.

[25] Richelieu on his deathbed was asked if he had any enemies he
wished to forgive. He replied that he had no personal enemies, although he had known some enemies of the state. Since he said no

ished is as likely to invite their repetition as to pardon and remit them. There are many men whose ignorance is so great that they consider it is sufficient to correct a given evil by forbidding its repetition. But such a view is so much in error that I can say with certainty that in such circumstances new laws are less remedies for public disorder than evidence pointing to the malady and proving the weakness of the government. It only indicates that if the old laws had been enforced there would have been no need either to renew them or to enact others in order to prevent new disorders which never would have occurred if a greater severity had been employed in punishing the misdeeds originally committed.

Ordinances and laws are completely useless if they are not infallibly followed by vigorous execution, and although in the course of ordinary cases justice requires authenticated proof, it is not the same with those which affect the state, because in such instances what appears to be circumstantial conjecture must at times be held sufficiently convincing, since plots and conspiracies aimed at the public welfare are ordinarily conducted with such cunning and secrecy that there is never any persuasive evidence of them until they strike, at which time they are beyond prevention. With such problems it is necessary sometimes to begin by punishing, but in all others it is necessary to have a clear determination of the truth

---

more on the subject it is assumed he had no thought of forgiving them.

supported by irreproachable witnesses and documentary
evidence. These maxims seem dangerous, and in fact they
are not entirely devoid of peril. But it is even more dangerous not to make use of them as the last and extreme
remedies in cases which can be established only by conjecture. One can do no more than retard the development
of a plot by such innocuous measures as the banishment
or imprisonment of suspected persons. A good conscience and thoughtful and judicious mind, knowing the
course of affairs, the future almost as surely as the present, will be on its guard against the possible bad consequences, while lesser men will see the effectiveness of
such punishment. At the very worst, the abuses which
can be committed will injure only private individuals,
which really has little bearing on the matter and should
not be taken too seriously, since their interests are hardly
comparable to those of the state. Nevertheless it is necessary to be very careful in such an instance not to open
the door to tyranny by these means, which will indubitably be avoided if, as I have suggested above, only mild
remedies are used in doubtful cases.[26]

Punishments are so necessary for violations of the public interest that it is not allowable in such cases to base
indulgence upon a prior record of good performance,
that is, to overlook a misdeed because he who has com-

[26] Even Richelieu seems to be troubled by the implication of
this maxim—a perennial temptation to men of action. Nevertheless, he did not hesitate to follow it.

mitted it has performed a notable service at some earlier time. That is, nevertheless, what had often been practiced in this realm up to my time, where not only little breaches had been forgotten in consideration of past services of importance, but the greatest crimes had been completely overlooked in return for services of no consequence, which is completely insupportable. Good and evil are so different and so opposed to each other that they never should be put in competition. They are two enemies between which no quarter should be asked or given. If the one is worthy of reward, the other is deserving of punishment. Each should be dealt with according to its merit.

While conscience could allow a good deed to go unrewarded or a serious crime without punishment, reasons of state could never permit either. Punishments and rewards concern the future more than the past. It is absolutely necessary for a prince to be severe in order to avoid misdeeds which might be attempted in the hope of obtaining clemency if he were known to be an easy prey to indulgence. It is necessary that he recompense those officials most useful to the public administration, both by encouraging them to continue to do well and by holding them up as examples for everyone to imitate and follow. It would be a pleasure to pardon a crime if by so doing one did not have reason to fear bad consequences, and the necessity of the state might sometimes legitimately preclude the recompensing of a service, if in depriving those involved one did not kill all hope of future rewards.

Noble souls take as much pleasure in doing good as they find it painful to be severe, and I end my discourse on punishments and penalties in order to finish this chapter more agreeably on benefits and rewards.[27] In this regard I can only state that there is a difference between the gifts which are made in recognition of services and those which have no foundation save the favoritism of kings. The latter should be sharply lessened, while the former should have no limits other than those of the public services performed.

The well-being of states indisputably requires their princes to be liberal, but I have more than once noted that there are rulers who by their natural bent are not inclined to be generous. I have always felt that such a fault, blameworthy in any person, was a dangerous imperfection when found in a sovereign. By title he is called upon to be something of an image of his Creator, Who by His nature does good to everyone. A ruler cannot fail to imitate Him in this respect without being held responsible to Him. The reason for this is that He wishes sovereigns to take pleasure in following His example and distribute their favors handsomely. On the other hand, those who give grudgingly are like misers who, providing their banquets with good meat, prepare it so poorly that neither those who share nor those who do not

[27] About which, however, he has remarkably little to say.

share in the expense of the food have any pleasure in the meal.

I would dwell at length on this subject if I had not already spoken of it in an earlier chapter, when discussing how important it is that princes reward those of their councillors who serve them faithfully.

CHAPTER VI

THE NEED FOR CONTINUOUS

NEGOTIATION IN

DIPLOMACY

States receive so much benefit from uninterrupted foreign negotiations, if they are conducted with prudence, that it is unbelievable unless it is known from experience. I confess that I realized this truth only five or six years after I had been employed in the direction of your affairs. But I am now so convinced of its validity that I dare say emphatically that it is absolutely necessary to the well-being of the state to negotiate ceaselessly, either openly or secretly, and in all places, even in those from which no present fruits are reaped and still more in those for which no future prospects as yet seem likely. I can truthfully say that I have seen in my time the nature of affairs change completely for both France and the rest of Christendom as a result of my having, under the authority of the King, put this principle into practice—something up to then completely neglected in this realm.

Some among these plantings produce their fruits more

quickly than others. Indeed, there are those which are no sooner in the ground than they germinate and sprout forth, while others remain long dormant before producing any effect. He who negotiates continuously will finally find the right instant to attain his ends, and even if this does not come about, at least it can be said he has lost nothing while keeping abreast of events in the world, which is not of little consequence in the lives of states.

Negotiations are innocuous remedies which never do harm. It is necessary to act everywhere, near and far, and above all at Rome. Among the three items of advice which Antonio Perez [28] gave to the late king, he placed first that of making His Majesty appear powerful at the papal court. This was not without reason, since the ambassadors of all the princes of Christendom present there judge that those who are treated by that court with respect and as having authority are in fact those actually most powerful. In truth their judgment is not badly founded, for while it is certain that there is no one in the world who should have greater respect for reason than the pope, yet there actually is no place where power is more highly rated than at his court. This is made clearly evident by the fact that the respect rendered there to ambassadors of princes rises and falls day by day accordingly as the affairs of their masters wax or wane.

[28] Antonio Perez (1534–1611), secretary to Philip II of Spain, from whose wrath he fled in 1591, finding refuge at the court of Henry IV of France. It was mainly from his venomous pen that the world derived the commonly accepted harsh portrait of Philip.

Indeed, it often occurs that ministers receive two contradictory treatments on the same day if a courier who arrives in the evening carries different news than the one who came in the morning.

States correspond to the human body. A good color in a man's face leads the doctor to conclude that there is nothing seriously wrong inside, as that good appearance arises from the sound condition of the internal organs. By the same token it is certain that the best means which a prince can employ to stand well at Rome is to put his own house in good order. It is almost impossible to have a great reputation in that city, which has long been the diplomatic and geographical center of the world, without everywhere enjoying great advantage to our interests.

Common sense teaches us that it is necessary to watch our neighbors closely, because their proximity gives them the chance to be bothersome. But it also puts them in the position of serving as the outposts preventing the close approach to our walls. Mediocre minds restrict their reach to the confines of the state in which they were born. But those to whom God has given more intelligence, learning from doctors that with the most serious diseases the manifestations are more visible at the extremities, omit nothing which can fortify them thoroughly against any eventualities.

It is necessary to act in each instance, I should point out, according to the particular circumstances and with means appropriate for those with whom one is negotiating. Different nations have different characters, some quickly carry out what they have in mind, while others walk with feet of lead. Republics are in this latter category. They proceed slowly and one ordinarily does not get from them at the first attempt what is sought. Rather it is necessary to be content with little in the hope of getting more later. For this reason it is wise to negotiate painstakingly with them in order to give them time, and to press them only when they are ready for it.

It should be noted that while strong and convincing reasons are proper for presentation to men of power and genius, mediocre minds are more influenced by small points, since these are on their level of comprehension. Each person conceives of public affairs according to his own capacity; major problems seem easy to deal with to men of intelligence and self-possession, but those who do not have these qualities ordinarily find them formidable. Such people frequently are incapable of grasping the significance of what is proposed to them, occasionally missing its main point, and even sometimes emphasizing some aspect not meriting consideration.

In certain instances it is necessary to deal with each person according to the bent of his mind. Sometimes it is best to speak and act boldly, being first sure one has right on his side, which rather than causing a rupture is more likely to prevent it by smothering it before its birth. In other instances, in place of resenting the inappropriateness of imprudent remarks made by those with whom one

is treating, it is better to suffer them with both forbear-
ance and good appearance, having an ear only for those
remarks leading toward the end in mind. There are some
men so presumptuous as to think they should bluster on
all occasions, believing this to be a good way to obtain
what they could never acquire by reasonable persuasion
and what they know they could never get by force. They
think they have dealt a blow when all they have done is
to threaten to do it. In addition, such a stratagem, contrary to good sense, never succeeds with honorable men.

Just as ignoramuses are not good negotiators, so there
are certain minds so finely drawn and delicately organ-
ized as to be even less well suited, since they become
overly subtle about everything. They are, so to speak,
like those who break the points of needles by trying to
make them too fine. For the best results, it is necessary
that men hold themselves to a middle course. The most
successful ones use their keenness of mind to prevent
themselves from being deceived, having a care not to use
the same means for deceiving those with whom they are
negotiating. One is always suspicious of men who employ cunning. Those who give the impression of lacking
frankness and sincerity rarely advance their cause. The
same words often enough have two meanings, depend-
ing on the one hand on the good faith and openness of
men and on the other on their artfulness and subtlety.
For those employing the latter it is very easy to twist the
true meaning of a word into some preconceived inter-

pretation. It is absolutely necessary, therefore, to utilize as negotiators those people who know the weight of words and how best to employ them in written documents.

Important negotiations should never be interrupted for a moment. It is necessary to pursue what one has undertaken with an endless program of action so ordered that one never ceases to act intelligently and resourcefully, becoming neither indifferent, vacillating, nor irresolute. It is also necessary not to be discouraged by a bad turn of events, since it sometimes happens that the wisest undertakings produce unhappy results. It is difficult to fight often and always win. It is a sign of the greatest good fortune when success smiles on large undertakings and frowns only on those of which the outcome is of little importance. It is ideal when negotiations are so harmless that one can acquire great advantages from them without ever suffering any misfortunes. If someone should say that this is not often the case, I consent to his questioning of my judgment if he is able to find by careful observation that one can impute a given failure to the mode of conduct I have proposed rather than to the maladroitness of those who tried to carry it out. Even if it does no other good on some occasions than gain time, which often is the sole outcome, its employment would be commendable and useful to states, since it frequently takes only an instant to divert a storm.

The same is true for marriage alliances commonly con-

tracted between crowns, which do not always produce
the fruit desired of them. Nevertheless, they must not
be neglected, for they not infrequently provide one of
the most important keys to a given negotiation. They
always possess at least the one advantage that for a time
they foster the continued respect each party has for the
other, and even that much success justifies them. In order to have good fruit it is necessary to employ the art
of grafting. So also princes born to parents of high and
equal quality ought themselves for this reason to be of
high station, and it is indisputable that their blood will
preserve its distinction if not mixed with that of lesser
families. In addition, marriage alliances sometimes serve
to bind together leagues and other associations among
great powers, and, although they do not always produce
these good effects, the benefits of this nature which the
house of Austria has received from them show that they
are not negligible.

In matters of state it is necessary to profit from everything possible; whatever is useful is never to be despised.
Leagues are in this category. The fruits are often very
uncertain, but they must not be ignored. It is true, however, that I would never advise a great prince to embark
voluntarily on the founding of a league designed for
some difficult objective unless he is strong enough to
carry it out alone should his allies decide to desert him.
Two reasons lead me to this conclusion. The first is based
on the weakness of unions, which are never too secure

when headed by several sovereigns. The second consists
in the fact that lesser princes are often as careful and
diligent in involving great kings in important commit-
ments as they are feeble in aiding them, although they
are fully obligated to do so. They sometimes even put
themselves above obligations to those they have committed to the cause perhaps against their will.

Although it is a common saying that he who is strong
ordinarily is right, it is at the same time true that when
two unequal powers are joined by a treaty, the greater
courts the risk of being abandoned by the lesser. The
reason for this is self-evident. His good reputation is so
important to a great prince that no possible gain could
compensate for its loss, which would be the result if he
failed to hold to his pledged word. But anyone can offer
terms to him of little power which he will probably consider, in spite of his sovereign rank, more useful than the
retention of his honor, and thus lead him to evade his
responsibility to his partner. The latter, although fore-
seeing the disloyalty, can do nothing to prevent it because to be abandoned by one's allies is of lesser consequence than the loss of prestige that would come from
a violation of one's word. Kings should be very careful
with regard to the treaties they conclude, but having
concluded them they should observe them religiously. I
well know that many statesmen advise to the contrary,
but without considering here what the Christian religion
offers in answer to such advice, I maintain that the loss

of honor is worse than the loss of life itself. A great prince should sooner put in jeopardy both his own interests and even those of the state than break his word, which he can never violate without losing his reputation and by consequence the greatest instrument of sovereigns.

The importance of my present task makes me remark that it is absolutely necessary to be discerning in the choice of ambassadors and other negotiators, and one cannot be too severe in punishing those who exceed their authority, since by such misdeeds they compromise the reputation of princes as well as the fortunes of states. The irresponsibility or corruptness of some minds is sometimes so great and the consuming ambition of others, who are neither weak nor bad, to accomplish something is often so keen that unless they are held within bounds prescribed for them in terms of fear and the threat of utter condemnation, there will always be some who allow themselves to be drawn into the making of a bad treaty rather than none at all. I have had so many experiences with this truth that before ending this chapter I must say that anyone who lacks the necessary devotion to the welfare of the state will fail to be rigorous in such matters.[29]

[29] Richelieu must have considered this chapter a summary of his own diplomatic policy. It hardly pictures him as seeking French mastery over Europe.

CHAPTER VII

THE NEED TO APPOINT

SUITABLE MEN TO

PUBLIC OFFICES

So many evils befall states because of the incapacity of those employed in the principal positions and most important commissions that the prince and those who have roles in the administration of his affairs need to exercise the greatest care in seeing that each public servant is charged only with those functions for which he is suited. The clearest minds being sometimes blind to what is close to them, and seeing that few men are willing to recognize their own limits, those who find themselves in the favor of princes almost always believe themselves worthy of all kinds of positions, and, on this false basis, they neglect nothing which could enable them to acquire them. However, it is true that such persons, although capable of public service in certain positions, are also capable of great mischief in others.

I have seen in my time such strange misfortunes come about from the poor selection of officials, that I am constrained to say something on the subject in the hope of forestalling their repetition in the future. If doctors do not allow new cures to be tried upon important people, it is easy to see how dangerous it is to put the principal offices of the state in the hands of people without experience, giving by this means a chance to apprentices to make experiments under circumstances which necessarily call for masters and skillful conduct. Nothing is more capable of ruining a state than such a procedure—an infallible source of all kinds of misfortunes.

An ambassador poorly chosen for the making of an important treaty can, by his ignorance, commit a great blunder. An army general incapable of performing his task can, by a wrong decision, risk the fortune of his master and the well-being of his country. A governor of an important region destitute of the attributes necessary for his office can, in an instant, so advance the ruin of all the realm that a century will be needed to repair his damages. I dare say, indeed, that if all those who are in public offices were worthy of them, their states would not only be free from many of the misfortunes which often trouble their tranquillity, but would even enjoy an immeasurable happiness.

I well know that it is very difficult to find subjects who have the qualifications required for the positions for which they are destined. But at least they should possess the basic characteristics necessary, and when one can find an accomplished man, there is not a little satisfaction in choosing the best that can be found in these sterile times. If the mask behind which most men ordinarily hide, if the artful ways with which they habitually disguise their shortcomings keep the truth from us until they are in high office, at which time they appear as bad as we had estimated them to be good when selected, it is necessary promptly to repair the error. And, if indulgence can at times tolerate some incapacity, it can never suffer malice, which is too prejudicial to the welfare of the state to be tolerated purely out of consideration for personal feelings.

In this regard it is necessary to impress upon kings clearly the degree to which they are responsible to God when they bestow the principal offices of state solely on the basis of favoritism. This can lead to their being filled by mediocre men, to the prejudice of the well-being of their states. It is necessary to point out at this juncture that while one should not condemn out of hand all personal attachments which have no other foundation than the natural affection one feels more strongly for one person than for another, one cannot excuse princes who allow themselves to be carried away to the point of giving to those they thus like responsibilities in the discharge of which they can be as detrimental to the interests of the state as they can be useful to their own.[30]

---

[30] Here is pointed up one of the great weaknesses in Louis XIII, against which Richelieu had to struggle to his dying day, both in his own behalf and against his potential rivals.

Those who are so fortunate as to have the good favor of princes by virtue of their personal appeal ought to be allowed to receive the benefits, even if they do not have the qualities which render them worthy, and the public has no reasonable right to complain unless they are vicious. But it is a sinister augury for a prince if he whose merit makes him an outstanding candidate is not considered because favor turns to look elsewhere. States are never in a worse position than when the partiality which the prince may have for a particular person rules out the services of those who would be the most useful to the public. In such a case, neither the esteem of the sovereign, nor the love borne toward him, nor the hope of reward can any longer arouse devotion to his service. One remains, on the contrary, in a state of indifference toward good and evil, and all men neglect their duty out of envy, jealousy, or spite, because there is no one who believes he will ever be rewarded for performing it.

A prince who wishes to be loved by his subjects ought to fill his principal offices and the leading positions of dignity in his state with persons so highly esteemed by everyone that the source of the choices can be easily seen in their merit. Such men should be looked for throughout the state and not appointed as a result of importunities or chosen from among the crowd more concerned with pressing at the door of the king's cabinet or those of his favorites than with serving the state. If favoritism played no part in the selection of public officers and merit were the sole basis, the state would find itself well served. In addition, princes would avoid much of the ingratitude which often arises in people little aware that the benefits they have received have not been earned. It is, needless to say, the qualities that the latter lack which make able men capable and desirous of acknowledging their obligations. Many show the proper sentiments at the moment of being favored. But their make-up is such that they soon easily forget their obligations to others since they are concerned only with themselves. As fire consumes everything it touches, so they approach matters of public interest only with a view to converting them to their private advantage, and at the same time despise both those who would do them good and even their countries. Favoritism can play an innocent enough role in certain instances. But a realm is in a bad state if the throne of that false goddess is raised above that of reason. Merit should always tip the scales, and if justice is on its side, favoritism cannot prevail without injustice.

Favorites are especially dangerous because those elevated by fortune seldom are influenced by reason, which is not useful to their ends. And fortune, alas, is ordinarily completely powerless to stem the course of those plans which are detrimental to the state. I must confess that I know of nothing so capable of ruining the most flourishing realm in the world as the appetites of such men, or the destructive influence of a woman in possession of a prince. I present this matter so boldly because there

are no remedies for this kind of evil except chance and
the passage of time, which left to themselves often allow
the patient to die without giving him any help, making
them the worst doctors in the world. The brightest light
cannot make the blind man see his way, nor can any
amount of reasoning open the eyes of a prince who is
blinded by favoritism and passion.

He whose eyes are so blinded can make good appointments only by chance, and since the welfare of the state
requires that they be made on a basis of reason, it is necessary that princes should not be the pawns of their favorites, who would deprive them of the open-mindedness
they need when dealing with the business put before
them. When the hearts of princes are held in such ways,
it is almost useless to try to do well, because the artifices
of those who are the masters of the royal affections twist
the meaning of the purest motives and often interpret the
most signal services as being offenses. Many princes have
been utter failures because they have preferred their private affections to the public interest. Misfortunes of this
sort have come for several princes because of the excessive and uncontrollable passion they have had for
women.

There are others who have fallen into equal trouble
because of a natural but blind affection for favorites
whose fortune they have raised to the ruination of their
own. There are still others who although they have no
natural attachments have been moved to extreme meas-

ures in favor of particular individuals, to their own great detriment. One can perhaps be astonished at this situation but its explanation is as easy to grasp as it is true if one considers that such practices result from the sickness of a mind which is agitated by an affection, and that the cause of the ensuing fevers is the corruption of the humors. One can thus say that this sort of violent attachment is more the fault of him in whom it is found than a result of the artfulness of him who receives the benefit. The evils of favoritism ordinarily carry their remedy with them, and the attachments, being violent, are of short duration. But if they are long continued, like fevers of that nature they often terminate in either death or an impairment of health that cannot subsequently be corrected except with the greatest difficulty. The wisest princes have avoided all evils of this sort by so managing their affections that reason alone has been their guide. Many have been cured after having learned from sad experience that without such guidance their ruin would be inevitable.

To return to the precise question proposed for this chapter, which was to demonstrate how important it is to discover those who are best suited to public positions, I will finish by saying that since the private interests of men are what usually induce them to make improper use of the responsibilities with which they have been charged, churchmen are often preferable to many others, particularly when the highest offices are considered. This is not because they are immune to personal interests, but because they have less than other men, since having neither wives nor children they are free of the attachments which have the most influence.

CHAPTER VIII

THE EVILS OF FLATTERY

SLANDER AND

SCHEMING

There is no plague more capable of ruining a state than the host of flatterers, slanderers, and people preoccupied with forming cabals and intrigues at court. They are so industrious at spreading their venom in various insidious ways that it is difficult to avoid it unless one takes the greatest of care. Since they have neither the social qualifications nor the merit to entitle them to a role in government, nor are serious enough to be concerned with the public interest, their only aim is to cause trouble. Thinking thus to gain much from creating confusion, they leave no stone unturned in spreading their flatteries, schemes, and slanders, thereby upsetting law and order. This, to be sure, deprives them of all hope of advancement on a basis of merit such as one might expect in a well-run state, but for them no such hope ever contained the likelihood of fulfilment anyway. In addition, it is a common thing for those not concerned with something to try to ruin it. There are no evil deeds that such men who are capable of doing no good, are not above trying, and there are not enough precautions that princes can take against their malice, which disguises itself in so many ways that it is often most difficult to protect oneself.

It often happens that there are those who though destitute of real feeling and intelligence, can create a semblance of them and feign a natural-appearing firmness together with a serious and profound wisdom, making themselves look good by criticizing what everyone else does even when most worthy of praise and it is impossible to do better in the matter criticized. There is nothing easier than to find obvious reasons for condemning something which no one could do better and which has been undertaken on such a solid basis that to have not so done would have been to make a gross mistake. Others, having neither mouths nor spurs, disapprove by gesture, head-wagging, or glowering grimace of what they dare not condemn with words or dispose of with solid argument.

To avoid flattery, when it is a question of dealing with such men, it is not enough for princes to deny them their ears. It is necessary to banish them from both the cabinet and the court, because sometimes so great is their facility that for them to speak to princes is to persuade them. Even when they cannot be persuaded they can leave an impression which in time has its effect, particularly if the same artifice is employed again. In addition, they take such little interest in the business of state that their judgment in such cases is more often based upon the number of witnesses than upon the weight of the accusations. It would be difficult for me to recall all the misfortunes of which such evil characters have been the authors during Your Majesty's reign. I have had so firm a resentment against such attacks upon the public interest that I am constrained to say that it is necessary to be without pity toward such men and to get rid of them promptly to prevent such misdeeds as some of those which have occurred in my time.

No matter how firm and constant a prince may be, he cannot without great imprudence and without exposing himself to his own ruin keep evil men near him. They can surprise him at an unguarded moment, as during the plague a malignant vapor seizes in an instant the heart and the brain of the most robust men when they think themselves to be in full health. It is necessary to drive out these public plagues and never allow them to return, unless they have disposed of all of their venom. This is so infrequently the case that the care we ought to have for peace more obliges us to continue their banishment than charity can urge their recall. I firmly advocate this view because I have never seen any of those lovers of factions and brewers of intrigues at court lose their evil ways or change their nature except when they have completely lost the power to do evil. To speak accurately, this is no change at all, since the desire to do evil still remains in them, while the means are gone.

I well know that occasionally one of these evil characters can be sincerely converted, but experience has
taught me that for every one who remains truly re-
pentant, one hundred return to their evil ways. I have
firmly concluded that it is better to be unrelenting
toward an individual worthy of forgiveness than to expose the state to certain danger as a result of having been
too indulgent either toward those who, disguising the
malice in their hearts, make only a disingenuous confession of their faults, or toward those whose light-headedness should give rise to fears of fresh relapses worse than
the original ones. It is no wonder that angels never do any
evil, since they are confirmed in grace. But that men, accustomed to this kind of malice, should do good when
they are committed to evil is a form of miracle of which
the mighty hand of God alone is the true source. And it is
certain that a man of great probity would have much
more trouble existing in an era corrupted by such men
than would a man whose display of virtue they did not
fear because his reputation was not so pure.

One sometimes thinks it is good for kings to tolerate
evils that seem of little importance at the outset, but I say
that they cannot be too careful about uncovering and
suppressing at their origin even the smallest intrigues
they find in their cabinet or court. The greatest fires ordinarily come from little sparks. He who extinguishes
the latter does not realize how great a destruction he has
prevented. But if, in order to find out, he leaves them

unextinguished, while the same causes do not always produce the same effects, he may find himself some time later in the predicament of no longer being able to stop what he has started. While it may be truth or only fable that a little fish can stop a great vessel although it could not make it go forward for an instant, it is easy to conceive from what naturalists tell us that it is necessary to be very assiduous in purging the court of those who can stop the progress of its undertakings even though they could never advance it. In such matters it is not enough to banish important men because of the power inevitably associated with them. It is necessary to do the same with lesser evildoers because of their maliciousness. All are equally dangerous, and if there is any difference the little men are more to be feared than the others because they are more covert.

So it is that bad air, as I have said, sealed in a coffer often infects a house, and the contagiousness which follows spreads to the whole city. It is just the same with cabinet intrigues, which often fill the hearts of princes with partialities that eventually trouble the bodies of their states. I can indeed say with truth that I have never seen troubles in this realm with any other origin, and I repeat again, it is more important than it seems not only to extinguish the first sparks of such conflagrations as soon as they appear, but even more to prevent them by banishing those who have no other thought but to ignite them. The well-being of the state is so important that one cannot deny it this protection without being held responsible to God. I have sometimes seen the court, in a period of peace, so full of factions in the absence of the practice of this salutary advice, that little more would have been necessary to overthrow the state. This knowledge, which is the same as that provided to Your Majesty by the history of similar perils, to which several and particularly the more recent of your predecessors have found themselves similarly exposed, has constrained you to have recourse to this remedy. And I have seen France so peaceful at home although it was at war abroad that to observe the general calm which the country enjoyed it would seem impossible that she was locked in combat with the greatest powers.

Possibly it may be said that the factions and discord of which I have just been speaking come more from the activities of women than from the malice of flatterers. But this does not rule out what I have said above, indeed it forcefully confirms it, since in speaking of flatterers and the like I have not meant to exclude women. They are more dangerous than men and of a sex to which are attached various kinds of attractions more powerful in exciting, confusing, and upsetting cabinets, courts, and states than the most subtle and industrious malice of men could ever hope to achieve. It is true that during the time Queens Catherine and Marie de Médicis directed the government of this country they had several women associated with them possessing great intelligence and

charm who accomplished indescribable evils, their
charms having won for them the most highly placed men
in the realm—and the most unhappy. They not only exploited such advantages to satisfy their passions; they
often conspired against those not pleasing to them because they served the state.[31]

I could pursue this subject further, but various considerations stem my pen, which is not capable of flattery
—indeed it openly condemns it. I cannot resist remark-
ing, however, that favorites, of which I spoke in the pre-
ceding chapter, often take the places of those whose
malice I have just been examining in this one. In addition
to these truths there is nothing left for me to say except
that it is impossible to guarantee absolutely that states
can be spared all the misfortunes that the kind of people
mentioned here can initiate, short of banishing them from
court, any more than one can keep a serpent at his breast
without exposing himself to the risk of being bitten.

[31] The references are respectively to Jeanne d'Albret (1528–72),
Queen of Navarre and mother of Henry IV, and Leonora Galigaï
(1571?–1617), wife of the ambitious favorite, Concini.

CHAPTER IX

THE POWER OF

THE PRINCE

Power being one of the things most necessary to the grandeur of kings and the success of their governments, those who have the principal management of states are particularly obliged to omit nothing which could contribute to making their masters fully and universally respected. As goodness is the object of love, so power is the cause of fear. It is certain that of all the forces capable of producing results in public affairs, fear, if based on both esteem and reverence, is the most effective, since it can drive everyone to do his duty. If this principle is of great efficacy with regard to internal affairs, it is of no less value externally, since both foreigners and subjects take the same view of redoubtable power and both refrain from offending a prince whom they recognize as being able to hurt them if he so wishes. I have said already that this power of which I speak should be based on esteem and respect. I hasten to add that this is so necessary that if it is based on anything else there is the grave danger that instead of producing a reasonable fear the result will be a hatred of princes, for whom the worst possible fate is to incur public disapprobation.

There are several kinds of power which can make princes respected and feared—it is a tree with various branches, all nourished by the same root. The prince ought to be powerful because of his good reputation, because of a reasonable number of soldiers kept continuously under arms, because of a sufficient revenue to meet his ordinary expenses, plus a special sum of money in his treasury to cover frequent but unexpected contingencies, and, finally, because of the possession of the hearts of his subjects, as we will clearly demonstrate.

A good reputation is especially necessary to a prince, for if we hold him in high regard he can accomplish more with his name alone than a less well esteemed ruler can with great armies at his command. It is imperative that he guard it above life itself, and it is better to risk fortune and grandeur than to allow the slightest blemish to fall upon it, since it is certain that the first lessening of his reputation, no matter how slight, is a step in the most dangerous of directions and can lead to his ruin.

· · · · · · · · ·

Those who guide themselves by the rules and precepts contained in this testament will without doubt acquire names of no little weight in the minds of both their sub-

jects and their foreign neighbors. This is particularly so
if, being devoted to God, they are also devoted to themselves; that is, if they keep their word and are faithful to
their promises. These are indispensable conditions to the
maintenance of the reputation of a prince, for just as he
who is destitute of them is esteemed by no one, so he who
possesses them is revered and trusted by all.

.   .   .   .

It is necessary to be deprived of common sense to be
ignorant of how important it is to great states to have
their frontiers well fortified. It is something especially
necessary for this realm where the light-headedness of
our people renders them incapable of making great conquests. On the other hand, their valor makes them in-
vincible in defense if provided with the proper positions
and facilities. These can give rein to their courage without exposing them to excessive hardships, the only enemies they find too difficult to conquer.

A well-fortified frontier is capable either of frustrating
the plans of envious enemies or at least of stopping the
course of their aggression if they should dare to try open
force. The temperament of our people needs to be pro-
tected from the terror which can arise from an unfore-
seen attack, a terror which can be forestalled by the
knowledge that the accesses to the realm have ramparts
so strong that they cannot be taken suddenly and can be
reduced at best only after considerable time.

.   .   .   .

There are no people in the world so little suited to war as ours.[32] Their light-headedness and impatience with the slightest difficulties are two characteristics which to my great regret only go to prove this. Although Caesar said that the Franks had mastered two techniques, the art of war and the art of talking, I must confess that up to now I have been unable to comprehend upon what basis he assigned the first of these attributes to them, since patience in work and suffering, indispensable traits in warfare, are found only rarely in them. If this latter characteristic did accompany their valor, the universe would not be big enough to limit their conquests. But while the courage God has given them fits them to conquer those who attack them, their light-headedness and inability to make a sustained effort render them incapable of dealing with an enemy who opposes delaying tactics to their impetuous ardor. From this comes the fact that they are not suited to conquests which require time, nor to the preservation of those which they are able to accomplish quickly. They are not only frivolous, impatient, and little accustomed to fatigue. In addition, one may accuse them of being unhappy with their lot and having little love for their country. This accusation is so well founded that one cannot deny that more of them fail to fulfill the obligations imposed on them by birth than is the case with any other people in the world.

[32] Doubtless written at some date after the serious military reverses of 1635 when France began her active role in the Thirty Years' War, this is Richelieu's famous indictment of the French soldier, often quoted by foreign critics and domestic reformers.

Although few men carry arms against their own prince, there is never a war against France but what Frenchmen are to be found on the enemy's side, and even when fighting for their own country they are so indifferent to the public interest that they make no effort to overcome their private whims. They run two hundred leagues to give battle, and are unwilling to wait a week for the best occasion; they get bored even before having to get to work. They do not fear danger, but they do not wish to expose themselves to any hardship. The least details are insupportable to them, and they do not have the fortitude to wait a single moment for their pleasure. They are even bored by continued success. At the beginning of a campaign their ardor is no less extraordinary, and indeed, at this stage they are more than men. But in a little while they relax until they become no more worthy than the common generality, and end up by getting more uninterested and softer than women. They always retain the courage to fight if one sees to it that they get into battle at once. They are, however, unable to await a better time, even though their honor, the reputation of their country, and the service of their master all require it.

They know neither how to draw advantage from a victory nor how to limit the success of a victorious enemy. In prosperity they are blinder than all other people, and lose both heart and judgment in time of adversity and drudgery. Indeed, they are subject to so many defects that some judicious observers, not without reason, have

been astonished at the fact that this monarchy has been
able to exist since its birth, seeing that although it has
always found faithful children to defend it, it has never
been attacked but what its enemies have found feudists
within who, like vipers, are ready to gnaw the entrails of
their mother. I well know that as a balance to these imperfections the French have many good qualities. They
are valiant, full of courtesy and humaneness; their spirit
is devoid of all cruelty and so free of rancor that recon-
ciliation is easy. But although these qualities are both an
ornament to civil life and essential requisites of Christianity, it is nevertheless true that being destitute of fortitude, patience, and discipline, they are like tempting mor-
sels served without the sauce necessary to make them
tasteful eating.

.   .   .   .

The former kings felt it so important to hold possession of the hearts of their subjects that some believed it
better to be king of the French than of France, and, in
fact, this nation at one time had such affection for its
princes that authors praised it for being ever ready to
shed its blood and risk its goods to serve them and the
glory of the state. Under the kings of the first, second,
and third races down to Philip the Fair,[33] the treasury of
the heart was the only one kept in the realm. I well know

[33] Philip IV (1268–1314). The first, second, and third "races"
were the Merovingian, Carolingian, and Capetian lines of kings
which successively spanned the whole history of France from the
fall of Rome to the French Revolution.

that bygone times have slight relation to or bearing on the present, that what was good in one century has little use in another. But although I realize that a treasury of hearts would not alone suffice now, it is also very certain that gold and silver are almost useless without it. Both the one and the other are necessary, and whoever lacks either will be in want in the midst of plenty.

CHAPTER X

CONCLUSION

In order to terminate this work happily it only remains for me to point out to Your Majesty that kings, being obliged to do many more things as sovereigns than they would have to do as private individuals, can never deviate even a little from their duty without committing more faults of omission than an ordinary person would be guilty of by commission. It is the same with those to whom sovereigns delegate a part of the powers of their governments, since this honor commits them to the same obligations as those possessed by their sovereigns. Both, when looked at as private individuals, are subject to the same faults as other men. But when one considers the public, for whose well-being they are responsible, their obligations are more numerous, for they cannot without sin fail to do any of the many things their offices charge them with. Thus it is that one who is both good and virtuous as a private individual can be a bad magistrate or sovereign because of the little regard he has for the ful-filling of the duties of his office.

In a word, if princes do not do everything within their power to keep in order the various classes in their states, if they are careless in the choice of members of their councils, if they ignore good advice, if they do not have a particular care to so conduct themselves as to appear the living embodiment of the law, if they are neglectful in establishing the reign of God, as well as of reason and justice, if they fail to protect the innocent, reward no-table public services and punish the disobedience and crimes which endanger the disciplined order and security of states, if they do not apply themselves to their utmost in trying to foresee and prevent possible evils and divert by careful negotiations the storms which the wind often can carry farther than one would think, if favoritism prevents them from choosing carefully those whom they honor with the highest offices and principal dignities of the kingdom, if they do not firmly hold the reins of gov-ernment with a view to giving the state the strength it ought to have, if on all occasions they do not give prefer-ence to the public interest over all private ones, though they otherwise be good, they find themselves much more culpable than those who transgress the laws and com-mandments of God either by commission or omission, it being certain, of course, that acts of commission and omission are really equally culpable.

I must also remind Your Majesty that if princes and

those who are employed under them in the highest offices in the realm have great advantages over private individuals, they possess such privileges only at a price, since not only are they exposed to the faults of omission I have indicated, but there are still others of commission, to which they are specially subject. If they use their power to commit acts of injustice or violence which they could not do as private persons, they have committed a sin of high office stemming from their authority, for which the King of Kings on Judgment Day will demand a special accounting. These two kinds of faults, peculiar to princes and magistrates, should well give them pause for reflection. They are considerably more serious than all those to which private individuals are heir because as universal causes rulers visit upon all those under their governance the effects of their misdeeds. Many in fact could save themselves as private individuals who damn themselves in their capacity as public persons.

One of the greatest of our neighboring monarchs, recognizing this truth, cried on his deathbed that he feared less the sins of Philip [34] than he did those of the king. His thought was truly pious, but it would have been more useful to his subjects and to himself if he had realized the importance of this at the height of his grandeur and public career rather than when he could no longer apply it to his rule, although it might still be useful for his salvation. I therefore beseech Your Majesty to think,

[34] Philip II of Spain (1527–98).

from this very moment, about what occurred to that great prince only at the hour of his death. As for myself, in the hope of convincing you of both its feasibility and its rightness, I promise that no day of my life shall pass without my making every effort to have the lesson involved prevail in my thoughts as I undertake the direction of the affairs of this realm which it has been your pleasure to entrust to me.